THE
CHRISTIAN
ANSWER

THE CHRISTIAN ANSWER

BY

PAUL J. TILLICH   THEODORE M. GREENE
GEORGE F. THOMAS   EDWIN E. AUBREY
JOHN KNOX

WITH AN EDITORIAL INTRODUCTION BY
HENRY P. VAN DUSEN

AND A FOREWORD BY
JOHN BAILLIE,
D.D.,
*Professor of Divinity in the
University of Edinburgh*

LONDON : NISBET & CO., LTD.
22 BERNERS STREET, W.1

First published in 1946

FOREWORD TO THE BRITISH EDITION
By John Baillie

ONE of the things that struck me most forcibly on revisiting the United States in the summer of last year was the unfamiliarity of the contents of the bookshops. Before the War I was about equally at home in the bookshops on both sides of the Atlantic, and I should say that three out of every four books displayed in New York and Chicago were at the same time being displayed in London and Edinburgh, and vice versa. Nor was I aware of any great change when I visited America early in 1941. Moreover, the change that has now taken place is largely one-sided. Most (though hardly so large a proportion as formerly) of the significant books appearing in Britain have continued throughout all the War years to be published in American editions ; but it is remarkable how small a proportion of the significant American books have lately been published in British editions.

The reason has of course been the acute shortage of paper and binding materials in this country, together with the want of labour in the printing and book-binding trades ; but the effect has been very regrettable—and most regrettable of all at a time when so strong a desire for a fruitful interchange of ideas has manifested itself in both countries. Our isolation has been accentuated by the greatly increased difficulty of seeing copies of the American journals, and by the irregularity with which these have reached us, so that we were often precluded not merely from reading the books but even from knowing their names and seeing them reviewed. It is in the field of philosophical, theological and religious literature that I can speak with most knowledge, and the hours I spent browsing last summer in these sections of the transatlantic libraries and book stores made me feel how real our loss has been.   I am therefore delighted that Messrs. Nisbet have seen their way to give us a British edition of the present most interesting volume.

The Christian Answer is as significant for the manner of its composition as for the ideas it contains.   As President van Dusen explains in his Introduction, it is the outcome of ten years of weekend discussions on the part of about twenty-five men and women who were united in their concern to understand the relevance of the Christian faith to the present world situation.   This kind of group discussion, with periodic meetings extending over several days, the participants being chosen with an eye both to the distinctiveness of their own contributions and to their readiness to profit from the contributions of one another, has been variously experimented with on both sides of the Atlantic during the last ten or fifteen years ; and it is probable that nobody, who has been privileged to have experience of it, can now doubt its fruitfulness.

Some of us now know, as we never knew before, what is meant by corporate thinking.   We have experienced the " encounter of other minds " in a far more challenging form than was possible in the ordinary atmosphere of debate, when the chief concern of each disputant was to get his own view accepted and the views of others triumphantly refuted.   And at the same time we have learned something about the meaning of fellowship.   In many cases such groups have not come out into the open with any united publication of the fruits of their thought ; they have been content with the more indirect, but very real, fruits manifest in the subsequent separate activities, both literary and practical, of their various members.   But this American

group, whom I first knew as the " Younger Theologians "
(though, as the Editor explains, they have now outgrown the appropriateness of that name), have put us
greatly in their debt by giving us a direct sample of their
results.

I am personally very grateful to them for having done
so, and I think there will be many to share my gratitude.
There are sections of this book that I have read several
times over, and mean to read again. I shall not say
what these sections are, but shall leave it to each reader
to find his own best bits for himself. I shall only say
that the pages to which I have found myself returning
are not those which are most like what I might myself
have written, nor even are they pages which, going
beyond anything I had already thought out for myself,
at once secured my agreement. Some of them are, on
the contrary, pages which have made me aware of this
or that important divergence (though within the frame
of an equally significant agreement) in the directions
recently followed by American and British religious
thought. And this has made me wish very much that,
instead of having British group discussions and American
group discussions, we could have an Anglo-American
group which would bring together interested people—
for weekends !—from both sides of the Atlantic. Perhaps
it is not too much to hope that before the *new* generation
of younger theologians in turn outgrow the appropriateness of such a name, the number of travel hours separating
the two countries will have suffered sufficient diminution
to give reality to this dream.

J.B.

Edinburgh,
March, 1946.

CONTENTS

INTRODUCTORY

THIS book is the outcome of an unusual process of preparation. It is informed by a quite definite purpose.

I

Just ten years ago, some twenty-five men and women —most of them teachers of religion, a few of them administrators and pastors—came together to consider issues of common concern in the interpretation of Christian faith for our day. The letter of invitation defined the character and purpose of their meeting : to furnish an occasion " for full, frank and leisurely exchange of ideas," in the hope that " by these discussions, the thought of all the participants will be greatly fructified, and they may discover a strengthening sense of unity as they go about their individual tasks."

That hope has been abundantly fulfilled. Through the past decade, the Group has met regularly for two weekends each year. Known initially as " The Younger Theologians "—a designation which the passage of time made inappropriate—they adopted the informal name " The Theological Discussion Group." Over the years, their discussions have canvassed the whole range of problems of Christian faith.

They began their work when religious thought, even within the Churches, was chaotic. In the realm of ideas, " Naturalistic Humanism," which had held the centre of attention during the preceding decade, had already spent its strength, and, except in limited circles, was no longer a major challenge to Christian faith. But it had left an aftermath of scepticism, relativism and uncertainty which was widespread. On the other hand, powerful counter-currents had set in, summoning men to a "return to orthodoxy." In the wider orbit of the world's life, most of the nations were in the grip of a depression which was spiritual no less than economic ; strident totalitarianisms were mobilizing the allegiance of millions ; and the international order was already clearly headed toward catastrophic conflicts.

In this situation, the achievement of agreement within a Group whose membership was deliberately chosen to embrace a wide sweep of theological and social outlook was hardly to be hoped for. Nevertheless, as time passed, an expectation hesitantly offered at the outset that " a group of people, united in a common vital concern for the Christian cause in our day, will be found to share a large body of common convictions—probably larger than any of them now realizes and richer than any of them has been able by himself to articulate " has been more than justified. Indeed the members of the Group have sensed a movement of conviction among them toward a consensus, none the less real because difficult to define, as to the character of the crisis which grips contemporary culture, as to the necessity of Christianity for its resolution, and even as to the essential answer of Christian faith to this crisis. Moreover, it has appeared to them that a somewhat similar consensus is gradually forming among the leaders of Christian thought generally, although it has not yet achieved definition.

Heretofore, no effort has been attempted to make the results of the Group's work available beyond its own members. Two years ago, however, they determined to press on to a possibility suggested in the invitation which first brought them together that, " should the venture justify itself, it is possible that some corporate writing might emerge from later discussions."

Employing the method which had already proved fruitful in their regular meetings, four members were asked to prepare preliminary papers on :

1. Diagnosis of the Present Situation (Why Take Christianity Seriously ?)
2. The Validity of Christian Belief (Is Christian Belief Intellectually Credible ?)
3. The Content of the Christian Gospel (What Has Christianity to Offer ?)
4. Christianity in Action (What Does Christianity Propose ?)

These preliminary statements were subjected to detailed scrutiny by the entire Group, and then returned to the writers for thorough redrafting. The second drafts were again criticized by the Group as a whole, and re-committed to the authors for further revision. The fourth topic was subdivided and Dr. Aubrey was asked to prepare a paper on " Christianity and Society." From that point, the work of final recasting has been carried forward through consultations and interchange of manuscripts among the five writers. This book is the result.

Thus, the chapters which follow seek to make articulate a consensus slowly formed over a decade in the corporate thought and discussion of two dozen men and women of widely different viewpoints and experience. They are the deposit of a thorough collaboration of the authors over a two-year period. In the latter phase, each con-tributor has submitted his colleagues' successive drafts to detailed criticism, and has had the benefit of similarly careful examination of his own writing. It must not be inferred that each of the writers would make fully his own everything that his colleagues say, but there is a general unity on basic propositions, and it may fairly be said that each chapter broadly reflects the convictions of all the collaborators. The entire membership of the

Theological Discussion Group cannot be held responsible for the chapters in detail, save as they are the fruit of a long and intimate corporate struggle to find the meaning of Christian faith for our time.

II

Moreover, this book has in view a particular audience. To its readers, it aims to present a forthright and vigorous challenge. It is directed primarily, though not exclusively, to thoughtful men and women who stand somewhat outside the Christian tradition, and yet are moved by the events of our time to inquire whether Christian faith may not hold truth and power which they have neglected and of which they and their world stand in need.

The writers of these pages are children of their generation. They have felt to the full the agony of its passage through World War, depression, premonition, and then global conflict renewed.

More than that, each of them has made his way along the intellectual and spiritual pilgrimage which is inescapable for the honest mind fully alive to the contemporary world of science and learning. The convictions here expressed are not simply an inherited legacy. Nor are they held in deference to any external authority. They have been hewn out by long and painful struggle of thought. Through such a process, the writers have been driven to the conclusion that Christian faith in its essential convictions is true, and that Christianity, despite the weakness and apostasy of the Churches, is indispensable to the reclamation of civilization. They invite others to face, as they themselves have done, both the inadequacy of alternatives and the adequacy of the Christian answer.

Finally, they are persuaded that these are issues upon which every intelligent and responsible person *must* press his way through to conclusions, and must face the choices which those conclusions demand. They believe that, in matters of faith as of politics, no neutrality is possible. " He who is not with us is against us." Not only in the relations of nations but in the life of every one of us, and here supremely, this is " a time for decision."

HENRY P. VAN DUSEN

NOTE ON THE AUTHORS

*T*HE *authors are all well-known figures in the American theological world. Dr. van Dusen, the Editor, who has just succeeded Dr. Henry Sloane Coffin in the presidency of Union Theological Seminary, New York, is almost equally well known on this side of the Atlantic both through the influential part he has played in ecumenical and missionary activities and through such recent books as* What is the Church Doing ? *and* They Found the Church There. *The writers of two of the essays are also now at Union Seminary ; Dr. Paul Tillich, who was in the first batch of distinguished German scholars to be ousted from their chairs in the German Universities by Hitler, and has now won a remarkable place for himself in America ; and Dr. John Knox who recently came from Chicago to succeed Dr. J. E. Frame in the Baldwin Chair of Sacred Literature. Dr. Theodore M. Greene of Princeton University now ranks as one of America's leading philosophers. Dr. George F. Thomas is Professor of Religious Thought in Princeton University and prominent as a philosophic theologian. Dr. E. E. Aubrey, a brother of the Rev. M. E. Aubrey, C.H., General Secretary of the Baptist Union of Great Britain and Ireland, is now President of Crozer Theological Seminary.*

THE CHRISTIAN ANSWER

I

THE WORLD SITUATION

By Paul J. Tillich

TO speak of a " world situation " is no longer, as it was even during the nineteenth century, a matter of daring anticipation or utopian vision. Two world wars within a quarter century reveal that " world " as an historical reality has come into being. " World " in the historical sense connotes such an interrelation of all political groups constituting mankind that events occurring in one section have direct repercussions upon all other sections. " World " in this sense, anticipated by a steady increase in world wide communication and traffic, world economic and political relationships, has existed since the First World War. The process has advanced with accelerating speed before and during the Second World War. To be sure, such a " world " exists only in the formal sense of the universal inter-dependence of all nations. As yet there is no unity of spirit, of culture, of organization, of purpose. Moreover, even the formal unity of the world is more apparent in the West than in the East, and the analysis which follows is necessarily mainly from the perspective of the Occident. Nevertheless, the forces which are transforming civilization are dominant not only in Europe and the Americas. They have penetrated from the West to the East, and not conversely, and have drawn Asia and Africa and Australasia also within a single revolutionary vortex. Therefore, it is not only possible but necessary to speak of a " world situation," to seek to discover the inner logic

and meaning of that situation, and to ask what message
Christianity has to offer to it.

I. GENERAL CHARACTER OF THE PRESENT WORLD SITUATION

The present world situation is the outcome—directly
in the West and indirectly elsewhere—of the rise, the
triumph and the crisis of what we may term " bourgeois
society." This development has occurred in three
distinguishable though overlapping phases. In the
first, the new society struggled to establish itself over the
remnants of a disintegrating feudal society—*the period of
bourgeois revolutions*. In the second, mainly through the
creation of a world mechanism of production and
exchange, the new society came to triumphant power—
the period of victorious bourgeoisie. In the third, mankind
struggles to regain control over the self-destructive
forces loosed by a regnant industrial society—*the present
crisis in civilization*. The disintegration and transformation of bourgeois society is the dynamic centre of
the present world situation.

1. *The first period* was marked by great political,
economic and cultural revolutions in Western Europe
and America. Feudalism and absolutism, both religious
and political, were crushed. The bourgeois way of life
became the determining, though not the only influential,
factor in Western civilization.

The guiding principle of this revolutionary period was
belief in reason. Reason did not mean the process of
reasoning, but the power of truth and justice embodied
in man as man. Man controlling nature and society
was the ideal born in the humanistic theory of the
Renaissance, ripened under the patronage of enlightened
authoritarianism, and brought to fulfilment through the
bourgeois revolutions. Reason was the very principle

of humanity which gives man dignity and liberates him from the slaveries of religious and political absolutisms. It is much more akin to the divine *logos* of the Stoics than to the manipulation of technical skills which won such triumphs in the second period of bourgeois society. The adoration of " Reason " as goddess in the French Revolution was a characteristic expression. The acknowledgment of every man as a rational being, capable of autonomy in his religious as well as his secular life, was the basis of the victorious struggle against the repressions of feudalism and every form of authoritarianism and tyranny.

In this struggle, out of which the modern world was born, one presupposition was always present, sometimes avowed, sometimes tacit. It was the belief that the liberation of reason in every person would lead to the realization of a universal humanity and to a system of harmony between individuals and society. Reason in each individual would be discovered to be in harmony with reason in every other individual. This principle of automatic harmony found expression in every realm of life. In the *economic* realm, it was believed that the welfare of all would be best served by the unrestrained pursuit by each individual of his own economic interests ; the common good would be safeguarded by the " laws of the market " and their automatic functioning ; this was the root-principle of the economy of *laissez-faire*. In the *political* realm, it was supposed that the political judgment of each citizen would lead automatically to right political decisions by a majority of citizens ; community of interest would assure sound democratic *procedures*. In the *international* realm, the play of interest among the nations would result in a comparatively stable balance of power between sovereign states. In the sphere of *education*, the essential rationality of human nature would produce, through free self-expression by each individual, a harmonious community. In *religion*, personal interpretation of the Bible and individual religious experience would follow a sufficiently uniform course among all believers to assure moral and spiritual conformity and to create and maintain a religious community of individual worshippers, the Church. Finally, this all-controlling idea found *philosophic* expression in various doctrines of pre-established harmony, those of Leibnitz, Descartes and their schools. The individual monad is a microcosm of the world. Ripening according to its own inner laws of logic, it develops in pre-established harmony with the whole of being.

This was the creed of the revolutionary movement in virtually all its intellectual and political leaders. Reality seemed to confirm it. Elements of automatic harmony could be discovered in every realm. The liberation of individual reason in economics and religion, in politics and education, did not bring on the disruptive consequences forecast by traditionalists and reactionaries. On the contrary, tremendous creativity was set free without the destruction of sufficient conformity to maintain national and religious communities. The enthusiastic belief in reason was vindicated by the prodigious achievements of mathematical science in the seventeenth century, by the development of autonomous national states after the disruptions of the Wars of Religion, by the establishment of natural laws in social and personal ethics. The law of harmony appeared to express the nature of reality. In the power of this belief, the new society overcame the resistance of feudalism and absolutism. In spite of all reactionary opposition, the nineteenth century may be regarded as *the period of victorious bourgeoisie.*

2. Reason was supposed to control nature, in man and beyond man, because nature and reason were held to be in essential harmony. But in the measure in which the bourgeois revolution succeeded, the revolutionary

impetus disappeared, and the character of reason as the guiding principle was transformed. The new ruling class could and did compromise with the remnants of feudalism and absolutism. They sacrificed reason as the principle of truth and justice, and employed it mainly as a tool in the service of the technical society they were bent upon perfecting. " Technical reason " became the instrument of a new system of production and exchange.

Technical reason provides means for ends, but offers no guidance in the determination of ends. Reason in the first period had been concerned with ends beyond the existing order. Technical reason became concerned with means to stabilize the existing order. Revolutionary reason had been conservative with respect to means but " utopian " with respect to ends. Technical reason is conservative with respect to ends and revolutionary with respect to means. It can be used for any purposes dictated by the will, including those which deny reason in the sense of truth and justice. The transformation of *revolutionary reason* into *technical reason* was the decisive feature of the transition from the first to *the second period of modern society*.

This displacement of revolutionary reason by technical reason was accompanied by far-reaching changes in the structure of human society. Man became increasingly able to control physical nature. Through the tools placed at his disposal by technical reason, he created a world-wide mechanism of large-scale production and competitive economy which began to take shape as a kind of " second nature," a Frankenstein, above physical nature and subjecting man to itself. While he was increasingly able to control and manipulate physical nature, man became less and less able to control this " second nature." He was swallowed up by his own creation. Step by step the whole of human life was subordinated to the demands of the new world-wide economy. Men became units of working power. The

profit of the few and the poverty of the many were
driving forces of the system. Hidden and irresponsible
powers controlled some parts of it, but no one the whole.
The movements of the mechanism of production and
consumption were irrational and incalculable. So it
became for the masses a dark and incomprehensible fate,
determining their destiny, lifting them today to a higher
standard of life than they had ever before known,
throwing them down tomorrow into utter misery and
the abyss of chronic unemployment. The decisive
feature of the period of victorious bourgeoisie is *the loss
of control by human reason over man's historical existence*. This
situation became manifest in the two world wars and
their psychological and sociological consequences. The
self-destruction of bourgeois society and its elaborate
scheme of automatic harmony is the characteristic of
the present period of transition.

3. Today the world stands in *the third phase of modern
history*, though in varying degrees in different countries
and continents. It has come to fullest expression in the
industrial nations of Continental Europe. In Anglo-
Saxon lands, it has thus far achieved a fairly successful
maintenance of the main features of the second period.
In Russia and parts of Asia, it has come to power before
the second stage had fully developed. These differences
must be borne in mind. Their neglect would falsify
the analysis and might lead to practical proposals which
would be foredoomed to frustration. Nevertheless, it
is possible to discern common structural trends which
characterize contemporary world society in its various
types. The dynamics of bourgeois society which have
precipitated the present world situation have been
dominant not only in the industrial nations of the
European Continent with their unbalanced economies,
but likewise in Britain, America and some smaller
European countries with their comparatively stable
situations, and also in Russia and the East where

resentment against the intrusion of dominating Western
exploitation has led to a leap from the first to the third
stage of modern social development, from a feudal and
authoritarian society to a totalitarian order.

In the third period which determines our world
situation, the foundation of bourgeois society has broken
down : namely, the conviction of automatic harmony
between individual interest and the general interest.
It has become obvious that the principle was true only
to a limited degree and under especially favourable
circumstances. Its validity was dependent upon certain
conditions—the continuing power of traditional values
and institutions strong enough to counteract the
disruptive consequences of the principle ; the increasing
strength of a liberal economy powerful enough to
counteract the inner contradictions of the system
through intensive and extensive expansion ; the
vestigial hold of feudal and absolutistic remnants
powerful enough to allay the transmutation of all social
life into a market-system. When these retarding and
disguising factors disappeared, the principle of automatic
harmony was revealed in all its patent insufficiency.
Attempts to replace it by a planned economy began.
" Rationalization " was invoked as a method of control
over the " second nature."

Totalitarianism was the first step in this direction.
One expression is the *Fascist systems*. They could achieve
partial success because they understood the breakdown
of the principle of automatic harmony and satisfied the
demand for a planned organization of the life of the
masses. In certain important respects, the Fascist
systems mark an advance beyond bourgeois society.
They have provided minimum security for all. They
have re-introduced unassailable authorities and commanding obligations. For these purposes they have
employed technical reason in the most effective manner.
But the Fascist systems could not succeed ultimately

because their basis was national, and thus they increased the disruption of mankind instead of uniting it according to the principle of reason. They destroyed any remnant of revolutionary reason and replaced it by an irrational will to power. Absolutism returned, but without the social, cultural and religious traditions which furnished solid foundations for the earlier absolute systems.

The other radical expression of the trend toward a planned society is the *Soviet system*. It could succeed for the same reasons which brought partial success to the Fascist systems. And it achieved an even greater security for the masses. Moreover, it has retained, at least in principle, revolutionary reason as an ultimate critical principle. But it also was a return to absolutism without the traditional foundations. It has come under the control of a bureaucracy which is inclined to replace revolutionary reason by technical reason after the pattern of the second phases of bourgeois society. Freedom for the individual is as completely lost as under the Fascist systems.

Both systems are reactions against the bourgeois faith in automatic harmony. Both are ambiguous : on the one hand, they attempt to bring the incalculable mechanism of world economy back under the control of man ; on the other hand, they aggravate the self-destructive forces generated by the second stage of bourgeois society. Both seek to elevate technical reason to " *planning reason* "—the characteristic feature of the third period and *the determining principle of our present world situation*.

The logic of bourgeois society in its struggle for survival is expressed in the development of reason from " revolutionary reason " through " technical reason " to " planning reason." This development must be held clearly in mind in every analysis of the present situation, in every question and answer regarding the future. This development cannot be reversed. We cannot return to a half-feudal absolutism. Neither the spiritual nor the economic conditions for such a return are present. We cannot return to the principle of automatic harmony epitomized in *laissez-faire* liberalism in economics. The political and social conditions for re-establishing the status quo have been destroyed by the present world catastrophe. And faith in automatic harmony cannot be re-established among the masses for whom it has meant oscillation between war, boom, depression and war renewed through thirty years. We must go forward under the direction of planning reason toward an organization of society which avoids both totalitarian absolutism and liberal individualism. This is not an easy course to define or to follow. Repelled by the inhuman brutalities of totalitarian planning, we are tempted to seek a return to a more or less concealed *laissez-faire* solution. Or, disillusioned by the catastrophic discredit of the philosophy of automatic harmony, we incline toward some kind of absolutism. Our task is to find a way between and beyond these extremes.

A biblical symbol may aid us in this attempt. When Hobbes developed his theory of the absolute state, he had recourse to the figure of " Leviathan," the all-embracing portent which, in the interests of the state, swallows all elements of independent existence, political and economic, cultural and religious. Struggle against the Leviathan of late-mediæval authoritarianism was the genius of the bourgeois revolutions. But the revolutionaries did not foresee that Leviathan was able to assume another face, not less formidable though disguised behind the mask of liberalism : the all-embracing mechanism of capitalistic economy, a " second nature," created by man but subjecting the masses of men to its demands and its incalculable oscillations. Since the First World War, the demonic face of this Leviathan has been unveiled. The battle against the destructive consequences of this mechanism has led to the totalitarian

organization of national life, and Leviathan appears
again with a third face combining features of the first
and second faces. The struggle between Leviathan in
its second and third phases, and the effort of individuals
and groups to discover a way by which both of them
may be brought into subjection, furnish the basic
structure of the present world situation. Christianity
must give its message to a world in which Leviathan in
its different aspects threatens all human existence to
its very roots.

II.   THE PRESENT WORLD SITUATION AS REVEALED IN MAN'S CULTURAL LIFE

THE general character of the present world situation
determines every aspect of mankind's existence. In
each sphere of life, the underlying structure can be
recognized as directly or indirectly controlling. In
some realms, resistance against the general trend is
stronger than in others, but none is independent of the
determining factors.

Although social and economic forces are predominant
in our present world, the spiritual realm shows the traits
of the "triple-faced Leviathan" as clearly as the
economic sphere, and in certain respects more significantly. The mechanism of mass production and
distribution has had profound effects not only on
economic and political structures but also on the inner-
most centre of *personal life*, on the character of all human
communities, and on the aims and methods of *education*.
We begin therefore with an examination of man's
cultural and spiritual life, and return later to the
economic and political factors which are there disclosed
as more fundamental and determinative.

Personality and *community* in their interdependence are
the very substance and basis of all social structures.

The prophets of bourgeois society believed that

Church of St. Francis, Assisi

GIOTTO

St. Francis Renounces His Possessions

The Six Collection, Amsterdam

REMBRANDT

Portrait of Jan Six

Museum, Vienna

TITIAN

Portrait of Jacopo da Strada

The Metropolitan Museum of Art

SARGENT

Portrait of Henry. P. Marquand

victory over feudalism and authoritarianism would create both fully developed autonomous persons and true communities of those who had been emancipated to personal freedom ; the principle of automatic harmony seemed to guarantee a harmonious society. But in no realm did the disintegrative influence of bourgeois society become more obvious than in that of personality and community. The " rational " individual is separated from every other individual. Society replaces community ; co-operation replaces unity in a common reality.

We may take an illustration from *Art*. The æsthetic realm always furnishes the most sensitive barometer of a spiritual climate. " Art indicates what the character of a spiritual situation is ; it does this more immediately and directly than do science or philosophy. . . . Science is of greater importance in the formation of a spiritual situation, but art is the more important for its apprehension."[1]

If we study the portraits of *Rembrandt*, especially in his later period, we confront personalities who are like self-enclosed worlds—strong, lonely, tragic but unbroken, carrying the marks of their unique histories in every line of their faces, expressing the ideals of personality of a humanistic Protestantism. To compare these portraits with *Giotto's* pictures of St. Francis and his monks is to recognize the difference between two worlds. Giotto's Francis is the expression of a Divine power by which man is possessed and elevated beyond his individual character and personal experiences. So are all other figures in Giotto's paintings. Between Giotto and Rembrandt are the portraits of *Titian*—individual expressions of humanity as such, representatives of the greatness, beauty and power of man. The transcendent reality to which Giotto subjects all individuals, their actions and emotions, has disappeared ; but the unique

[1] Paul Tillich, *The Religious Situation*, Holt, 1932, pp. 53–4, *q.v.*

individual, as in Rembrandt, has not yet appeared. The personality which found its highest portraiture in Rembrandt's pictures is the personality of the early bourgeois spirit, still subject to absolute forces, still shaped by the Protestant conscience, but already standing by itself, independent alike of transcendent grace and of humanity. In these three painters, the development of the ideal of personality in the modern world finds classic expression.

If we take the long step to portraits painted since the middle of the *nineteenth century*, we are in still another world. Individuals with a highly developed intellectuality and strong will appear—the bearers of technical reason, the creators of large-scale world economy, of the great monopolies, the conquerors of the forces of nature and the anonymous directors of the world-wide mechanism of capitalistic society. Personality has become at once the ruler and the servant of Leviathan. Will-power and technical rationality are united, and thus the way is prepared for the Fascist type in which the last remnants of the classical and humanistic ideal of personality are completely lost.

In the time of Giotto, relation to transcendent reality gave meaning, centre and content to personal life. In Titian, belief in the divinity of the human and the humanity of the divine furnished the centre of meaning. In Rembrandt, the experience of life with its tragedy and its ultimate hope determined personal existence. But the person of the period of triumphant bourgeoisie was dominated by purposes without ultimate meaning and by sensations and actions without spiritual centre. It was a personality which could still use the traditions of the past for æsthetic enjoyment, but which was not shaped by them. This naturalistic personality was formed by the demands of modern economy, and by neither divinity nor humanity, even if humanitarian and religious obligations were retained in the form of the moral or conventional standards of the bourgeois era.

The principle of harmony between reason and nature had promised the harmonious development of personal life if only ecclesiastical and political restrictions were removed. It was supposed that each man's personal centre would organize all bodily and mental functions in meaningful unity. The ideal of personality as the actualization by each educated individual of all human possibilities displaced the ideal of participation by every man, whether educated or not, in a common spiritual reality which transcends him and yet at the same time gives him a personal centre. In this fashion, the majority of human beings, since they could not share in the realization of the individualist goal, were excluded from significant participation in the ideal. They were consigned to remnants of religious tradition, or to education in technical reason and conventional morals. But even in the privileged strata of society, the situation was not greatly different. Technical intelligence replaced humanistic reason. Prophetic minds of the nineteenth century saw this transformation taking place, and they foresaw its destructive consequences. But they could not prevent it. Despite their protests, the technical depersonalization of man spread, not only in Europe and America but all over the world.

But man is fully rational only on the foundation of, and in interdependence with, non-rational factors. Therefore the predominance of technical reason evoked a reaction by the vital forces in man. They arose and made themselves manifest in both theory and practice. Whether called " instinct " or " passion " or " libido " or " interest " or " urge " or " will to power " or " élan vital " or " unconscious ground," they cannot be denied. They make it impossible to transform man into a psychological mechanism with intelligence and adjus-

tability.   They revolt against control by merely
utilitarian reason.   The conventional veil concealing
the dynamic centre of living man has been torn aside.
" Élan vital " displaced the rational centre of early
humanism.

However, the vitalistic protest against the mechanization of man is as ambiguous as reactions against
Leviathan in other realms. These protests have changed
its face, but not its being. Consciousness, discovering
the unconscious, tries to bring it into servitude to its
own purposes.   Instead of suppressing it, as early
Victorian morals demanded, it elevates it into equality
with consciousness.   The " adjusted " personality
becomes a more perfect instrument of an all-controlling
will, surrendering itself with fanaticism to irrational and
unconditioned purposes.

The development of the modern idea of personality
in its main stages has had its parallels in the structure
of all *communities*, natural communities such as the
family, and historical communities such as the state.

In the *first stage*, represented by the pictures of Giotto,
every individual participates in a communal movement
created by loyalty to a transcendent reality. It is an
all-embracing community in which every individual,
both peasant and prince, is borne forward by the same
spiritual reality. In the life of the Renaissance, outstanding individuals are predominant.   They are
isolated, each in his own way representing general
humanity, dealing with one another in the relations of
a privileged society but no longer in terms of community.
The person of Protestant humanism is a member of an
active group united by common purposes—the defence
of pure doctrine, the struggle against absolutism, the
crusade for the establishment of the Kingdom of God.
This is a community, however, not on the basis of a
common ground of universal authority but on the basis

of common devotion to particular aims for which it is necessary to fight. The spiritual centre of this community lies in the future.

In the *second period* of bourgeois society, not only a common spiritual ground but a common spiritual purpose was lost. In consequence, the different forms of community disintegrated. The family disintegrated into individuals each of whom lives for himself in the service of the mechanism of society. Communities of workers were replaced by mass co-operation of a non-personal character. Patriarchal responsibility for the servant, his welfare and his loyalty, gave way to the relations of legal contract. Neighbourhood as a form of community lost its meaning. The national community recovered reality only when attacked, and lost it again when danger passed. Even the community of friendship was destroyed by the universal sway of competition. Bourgeois society in its second phase destroyed community because it destroyed any common foundation and any common purpose. The service of the mechanism of mass production is not a possible spiritual centre for community. It separates individuals from one another in spiritual loneliness and competition. It turns them into atoms in the service of mechanical processes. It is not based on a common idea but on the controlling economic and psychological necessity that each man subject himself to the mechanism. Thus communities disintegrate into masses. Masses have neither common ground nor common purposes. They are driven in their objective existence by the incalculable movements of the mechanism of production, subjectively by the laws of mass psychology. This was the main sociological feature of the second period of bourgeois society. Many keen observers during the nineteenth century noted the dissolution of personality into atoms and community into masses, and forecast the cultural and political self-destruction of society.

c

To be sure, the trends just described were never completely victorious. Pre-bourgeois groups and pre-capitalist attitudes survived. In Russia, the majority of the populace were hardly touched by the disintegration of community. In America, the Protestant humanist ideals of personality and community are still vital in large sections of the country. In Asia, the family system resisted bourgeois atomization. But all these forms are under continuous and advancing attack. The dissolution of family, of neighbourhood, of personal co-operation is rapidly progressing. Even more important is the fact that every attempt to halt the general process of mechanization was finally subjected to the mechanism against which it protested. For example, European youth-movements sought escape by fleeing to nature and emotional communion. But they were caught in the totalitarian movements and transformed into instruments of its authoritarian machinery. To be sure, individuals in these groups no longer felt isolated and lonely. They were organized and their every activity, thought and emotion was planned and prescribed. Often they became not dissimilar to the " fighting orders " in the earlier opposite transition from feudalism to freedom. These groups which now embrace the whole younger generation in Fascist and Communist countries are " commanded " communities, logically a contradiction in terms, but in practice a very effective method for overcoming the feeling of solitude which was so prevalent in the second period, much more effective than the invocation of solidarity in the labour movements of the nineteenth century. The new type of personality produced in these communities has its spiritual centre completely beyond itself in the collectivity to which it belongs. The individual has become the self-dedicated instrument of a controlling will— not the unconscious and half-resisting instrument of the " second nature " in large-scale capitalism. Unconditional surrender to an unconditionally accepted purpose, resignation of any kind of autonomy, fanatical devotion are features of their existence. These are consciously dehumanized groups of human beings, very different from the automatically dehumanized industrial masses of the nineteenth century.

Thus, in the *third stage* of the bourgeois development, the attempt has been made to re-establish community on the basis of anti-bourgeois doctrines through fighting groups fired by a fanatical will to a new order of life and forged into the unity which always characterizes the fighting period of any revolutionary movement. The question is whether a real community has been born in these groups, whether a new " we-consciousness " has arisen which can overcome the atomization of a mechanized society. The situation is as ambiguous as in all other realms. On the one hand, a great effort has been made to overcome the loneliness of the individual within an absolutely devoted community. On the other hand, the method employed in this attempt represents the most radical employment of mechanization in the service of the new idea. The struggle against the dehumanization produced by the mechanism of modern capitalism has used even more fully mechanized methods and has thus carried through the process of dehumanization to its logical end.

The disruption and transformation of personality and community were furthered, both consciously and unconsciously, by changes in the philosophy and methods of *education*.

Prior to the modern period, a principal aim of education had been the induction of persons into the living community and tradition of the Church. It was significant that education originated within the Church, was conducted mainly by the Church, and was impregnated with the presuppositions and aims of Christian faith.

Reason as the principle of truth demands education for and through reason for everyone, and the massive achievements in educational theory and practice in Western civilization are due to this creative impulse. Humanistic education aimed to actualize humanity in each individual. World citizenship was the social goal and classical humanism the shaping tradition. Religion was recognized as one element in the development of the humanistic personality, but not its ground or centre. This ideal had great power all through the *first period* of bourgeois society. It was set over against traditional ecclesiastical education and it produced many notable representatives of Christian humanism.

But this humanistic ideal for education could not touch the masses. It requires favourable circumstances which society provides for only the few—a large measure of economic independence, outstanding intellectual abilities, rearing within a tradition of culture, etc. Consequently, education for the masses could not follow this pattern. Either it was neglected as in England or was adapted to a more technical pattern as in Germany.

In the *second period*, the humanistic ideal of education lost its hold and was employed more and more as a decoration necessary for social prestige or for professional advantage. Vocational education for particular purposes increasingly replaced humanistic education for a perfect humanity. In subservience to the demands of technical reason, so-called "realistic" education based on the natural and technical sciences step by step supplanted education through the humanities. Meantime, technical education of the masses for the service of large-scale industry was extended and refined. "Adjustment" became more and more the principle of education, adjustment to the existing society. Everyone must receive public school education, everyone must learn those skills most useful for success in the mechanism of production, everyone must subject himself to the ideals and norms of the dominant system. For many, the main purpose of education became that degree of adjustment which prevents serious disturbance of the existing order by uncontrolled individual initiative or revolutionary group action. To be sure, this was often hidden to the educators as well as to those educated. Individual spontaneity was cultivated. Productivity was not suppressed but encouraged. Religious and humanistic traditions were appreciated and used. So it seemed to be a truly " liberal " education, faithful to the humanistic and Christian heritage. Actually, the cultural achievements of the past wove an idealistic veil over the nakedness of this education and hid the face of Leviathan who was its real master. They had lost their original significance, their power as the expression of human possibilities and ultimate realities. In the measure that education has been subjected to the mechanism of modern society, it has lost its relation to truth and justice and consequently any ultimate meaning. Thus it becomes a ready victim of various kinds of non-rational powers which seek to give it meaning.

This whole trend is clearly reflected in developments in specifically *religious education*. Religious education was originally introduction into the tradition, the faith, and the sacramental experience of the Christian Church. This was still true of the churches of the Reformation though emphasis upon individual experience had increased. In the early stages of the modern period, autonomous reason could use religion as an element in the full development of human personality. But the more radical types of bourgeois education excluded religious education or recognized religion simply as a subject of historical interest. Within the churches, religious education either sought to adapt itself to the demands of autonomous reason or cultivated seclusion from the dominant trends in the surrounding culture. If the method of adaptation was chosen, religious education tended to become more and more a means of confirming the ideals of bourgeois society with the authority of religious tradition. If seclusion was practised, religious education became more and more unacceptable to the younger generation. Indeed it created powerful resistance against both religious education and religion itself and thus prepared fertile soil for totalitarian education to pseudo-religions.

But education without a determining centre is impossible. Since the Church with its beliefs and symbols was no longer the agent of educational indoctrination, the nation or local community increasingly took its place. States or cities took over responsibility for education. The nation was the community whose life must be interpreted by the teacher. Its history, constitution and present needs were the realities to which the teacher must adapt the pupil. Many emotional elements such as language, home, landscape, friendships are tied up with it. The nation became the ideological centre which demanded absolute devotion though itself above criticism. Here, likewise, the way was prepared for the third phase.

Vacillation in educational method between the ideals of autonomy and adjustment has been brought to an end in the *third period*. Adjustment as complete subjection increasingly swallowed the autonomous elements of liberal education. The breakdown of belief in reason had created intellectual insecurity and cynicism. Bourgeois conventions which, in the period of victorious bourgeoisie, gave an impression of rational harmony had lost their power. In the totalitarian schemes, education became introduction into a fighting, and eventually ruling, group. Rational criticism is excluded.

Knowledge for its own sake is discounted. Everything is related to the ultimate purpose of the group. The individual must resign all personal autonomy beyond the life of the group. Education for death, the demonic symbol created by National Socialism, expresses this final form of education in the service of Leviathan. Although there may be little danger that controlled education of this extreme type will prevail widely after the overthrow of Fascism, it must be recognized that standardized communication through radio, movies, press and fashions tends to create standardized men who are all too susceptible to propaganda for old or new totalitarian purposes.

The ambiguous character of totalitarian education is obvious. On the one hand, it leads beyond sterile adjustment to the mechanism of the industrial system. It overpasses the emptiness of such an aim. It creates enthusiasm, devotion, even fanaticism. On the other hand, it sacrifices personal life and individual creativity, the remaining elements of reason and harmony, more completely than has ever happened before.

The Christian Answer to the educational problem must be given in unity with the answer to the problems of personality and community. Christianity achieves actuality in a community based upon the appearance of Ultimate Reality in a historic person, Jesus Christ. For Christian faith, this event is in a profound sense the centre of history. The community which carries the spirit of Jesus Christ through the centuries is the " assembly of God," the Church. But this Church follows upon an age-long preparation—a general preparation in all religions and cultures throughout the world and a special preparation in an " elect people." Accordingly, we must recognize not only the manifest Church but also a " latent " or " potential " Church existing everywhere and at all times.

Ideally, education should be introduction into this

Church, the interpretation of its meaning and the communication of its power. Such education would embrace humanistic, scientific and technical elements. But it would provide meaning and cohesion for them all. The more collectivist periods of history were right in holding an aim for education equally valid for everyone and bearing directly or indirectly on everything. They were wrong in limiting free development of individual and social powers by the spiritual centre toward which all education was oriented. The Christian answer to the present educational situation must point men toward such a community as is sufficiently concrete and commanding to claim the hearts of individuals and masses and yet also sufficiently transcendent and universal to embrace all human ideals and possibilities.

III. THE PRESENT WORLD SITUATION REFLECTED IN THE ECONOMIC, POLITICAL, AND INTERNATIONAL SPHERES

As already noted, it was the assumption of bourgeois civilization that, in the *economic realm*, the welfare of all would be best served by the unrestrained pursuit by each individual of his own interests ; the common good would be safeguarded by the automatic functioning of " laws of the market." This was the root principle of *laissez faire*.

As a matter of fact, there was never a time when the economy of *laissez-faire* was in complete control. Since the beginning of the present century, a trend away from its rigorous application has been observable. State support and regulation more and more supplemented the operations of a free market. The necessity for such interference has become increasingly obvious since the First World War and especially in the days of the last great depression. Even in America, the insufficiency of liberal individualism for a large-scale economy under the dominance of rapid technical progress has become apparent.   Economic crises become more frequent, more widespread, more disastrous.   Chronic unemployment with its attendant misery and despair for large sections of the population, intolerable insecurity and fear for others, the dehumanizing effects of life bereft of meaning and hope for many—all these revealed the fundamental illness of the capitalist economy.   At the same time, failure to maintain a sound balance between the potentialities of production and the demands of consumption, and the necessity of bolstering private enterprise to prevent total collapse argued to the same conclusion.   A revolutionary situation emerged.   In more critical moments when the threatened breakdown of large industries endangered the whole national economy, even the most ruthless individualists in Big Business sought state intervention.   In these moments, they welcomed the " socialization of their losses," though in the next moment, when the immediate danger had passed, they vigorously opposed any attempt by the state to create conditions which might forestall a recurrence.   The present phase of economic development is determined primarily by state interference with the self-destructive mechanisms of the capitalist economy.

But state intervention was in most cases an ambiguous device : on the one hand, it saved the monopolistic system from complete collapse ; on the other hand, it produced resentment in those who were saved by it because it limited their free use of economic power.

State interference was a half-way measure which, in the long run, could not survive.   In Fascist countries, its contradictions were solved by an amalgamation of the leading monopolies with the state, and the dictatorial administration of both of them, though without abolition of private ownership.   In Russia, private ownership of industry was completely abolished and the entire economy is dominated by a bureaucracy interested in furthering production and in the prestige and power associated with it, but not in private profits. In the United States, on the other hand, state interference has induced a growing reaction against the managing bureaucracy and a strong trend back toward industrial autonomy. In Great Britain, public opinion oscillates between the two extremes and seeks a third way in terms of an all-embracing scheme of social security with the maintenance of capitalist ownership. In the meantime, the economies of all countries have been brought into complete subservience to centralized war administrations.

The basic question in the present situation is : Shall mankind return to the monopolistic economy from which our present economic, political and psychological disintegration has resulted ? Or shall mankind go forward to a unified economy which is neither totalitarianism nor a war expedient ? If the former rulers are able to effect the first course against the demands of the masses for security, a re-enactment of the history of recent decades leading to a final catastrophe can be forecast. On the other hand, if the masses are powerful enough to force their way forward against the vested strength of the traditional rulers, the question will arise as to how a rational organization of world economy can be developed without the creation of a mechanism as oppressive as the " second nature " created by capitalism. In summary, how can security and a decent standard of life for all be attained according to the infinite productive power of mankind, without the complete mechanization and dehumanization of man ? This is the question to which Christianity must seek to bring an answer.

Christianity cannot offer technical advice for economic planning, but that is not necessary. According to leading economists, the economic problem can no longer be regarded merely as a problem of perfecting economic techniques. The technical aspects of planning for stability and efficiency have been explored in all directions, both theoretically and practically. The problem of an economic system able to give security of permanent full employment and certainty of decent livelihood for all is much more largely in the realms of political and moral decisions. It is in the realms in which religious principles are decisive. Christianity can insist that the virtually infinite productive capacities of mankind shall be used for the advantage of everyone, instead of being restricted and wasted by the profit-interests of a controlling class and the struggle for power between different groups within that class. Christianity should reveal and destroy the vicious circle of production of means as ends which in turn become means without any ultimate end. It must liberate man from bondage to an incalculable and inhuman system of production which absorbs the creative powers of his soul by ruthless competition, fear, despair and the sense of utter meaninglessness. Christianity must denounce equally a religious utopianism which talks about abolishing the profit motive by persuasion in order to evade necessary social transformation, and a religious escapism which proclaims a transcendent security of eternal values in order to divert the masses from their present economic insecurity. At the same time Christianity must reject totalitarian solutions of the economic problem in so far as they destroy spontaneity in the relations between man and his work and deprive the individual of his basic rights as a person. Christianity must support plans for economic reorganization which promise to overcome the anti-thesis of absolutism and individualism, even if such plans imply a revolutionary transformation of the present social structure and the liquidation of large vested interests.

Politics and economics cannot be separated. They are interdependent.

Democracy was the weapon with which the fighting bourgeoisie conquered absolutism. It was, however, a limited democracy. In England up to the present century, it was limited by restrictions as to the right to vote and by an aristocratic and exclusive system of education for and election to political leadership. In France after the Great Revolution, it was limited by the device of a census designed to safeguard the bourgeois upper classes against participation in the control of the nation by the disinherited masses. In the United States, it was limited by the tradition of a two-party system which prevented the industrial classes from becoming an independent political power and, in the South, by a poll-tax which prevents the masses from influencing policy. In Imperial Germany, the power of conservative Prussia and of the King-Emperor were effective checks upon the autonomy of the Reichstag. Alongside these limitations on democratic procedure, there were important outlets for the rising pressure of the masses—in America, the frontier and the inexhaustible resources of a continent ; in France, the dominance of the petty-bourgeoisie and an incomplete industrialization ; in Germany, a rapidly rising standard of life ; in Britain, the colonial empire and shrewd adjustment by the ruling classes to the needs of the hour.

Today, the situation has changed, partly through dislocation in the factors which made effective democracy possible, partly under rising pressure from the masses who have become restive under the impact of recent political and economic catastrophes and demand full participation in democratic processes. In large sections of the world, democracy has never existed. In many countries where it existed in varying degrees of strength, it has been destroyed. In still others, it has been saved by drastic modifications in original theory and practice. In all democratic countries, a marked anti-democratic trend is noticeable. There are three main expressions of this trend toward new forms of political life. In one, a single party attempts to gain totalitarian control over the entire nation, abolishing any democratic check upon its use of power—the Fascist type. In the second, aristocratic and monopolistic elements seek to strengthen their control by undermining democratic methods and a democratic faith—the reactionary type. In the third, a democratically established bureaucracy achieves more and more independence and creates the tools for a planned reorganization of society ; the New Deal is representative of this type. By recourse to such measures democracy seems to be saved very much as capitalism was temporarily saved by recourse to state interference.

All these varied developments prove that the theory of liberalism has as limited possibilities in politics as in economics. It can work only under comparatively favourable conditions. Democracy presupposes a natural harmony between the different interests and, therefore, the likelihood of a satisfactory balance between them. When this balance is destroyed, democracy no longer works. More particularly, democracy is successful so long as the interests of different groups are harmonious to such a degree that the minority prefers acceptance of the majority decision to a revolutionary effort to overthrow it. When the point is reached where the minority no longer accepts the majority decision, democratic procedures fail. This may happen through the initiative of revolutionary groups from below or of reactionary groups from above or, in the case of Fascism, by an alliance of revolutionary and reactionary elements at the middle.

The great political question which emerges in the present situation is : Can we return to democratic institutions which have been partially abolished, by the development of democracy itself? Can we turn backward while facing the gigantic task of reconstructing a world in ruins with millions of human beings at the limit of a tolerable human existence? If it is not possible to go back, must we go forward to a centralized world bureaucracy? Would that not mean the end of democratic procedures everywhere? and would that, in turn, not involve the exclusion of the common people from the establishment of a world which is supposed to be their world?

In seeking answers to these questions, a first requisite is to recognize the ambiguity in the term " democracy." *Democracy as a constitutional procedure* for the establishment of government is a political form which embraces a great variety of methods. It must be considered as a means to an end but not as an end in itself. It can be employed as long as it works successfully and no longer. *Democracy as a way of life* which does justice to the dignity of every human being is the basic principle of political ethics. But it may be that democracy in the latter sense can be realized only by a limitation or transformation of democracy in the first sense. Jefferson's prophecy that democratic procedures will work only as long as differences in power and property are not too great has been vindicated. New methods are demanded in order to save " the democratic way of life " in the ethical and religious sense. Such methods must effect a planned organization of society which is neither Fascist nor reactionary. *Christianity* must support them as it must support corresponding plans for social security and a higher standard of life. Christianity must support both, not by technical or legal suggestions, but primarily by the creation of a new community which can find expression in political forms. Christianity must not identify itself with any particular political form, whether feudalism or bureaucratic patriarchalism or democracy. It cannot sanction democratic forms which disguise the destruction of community and personality. It cannot accept the double-faced Leviathan whether he presents himself through democratic or authoritarian structures. Christianity must declare that, in the next period of history, those political forms are right which are able to produce and maintain a community in which chronic fear of a miserable and meaningless life for the masses is abolished, and in which every man participates creatively in the self-realization of the community, whether local, national, regional or international.

Thus the problem of *international relations* is raised.

The present international situation shows one fact with unchallengeable finality : The division of the world into a large number of states, each possessed of unlimited sovereignty and right of self-determination, does not effect what was expected of it—a balance of power according to the principle of automatic harmony. The present international situation, not less than the economic and political situations, is the definitive refutation of that principle. This is true not only of Continental Europe where it is most obvious but also of the Americas and Asia and the Middle East. It is true of all sections of the world, just because today *world* is a historical reality.

Balance of power was the obvious principle for relations between nations at a time when the unity of the Holy Roman Empire had disintegrated and a number of independent sovereign states had appeared. Just as in economics and politics the former bases of unity were replaced by the theory of automatic harmony, so in the world scene the religious cohesions were replaced by the assumedly automatic harmonies of sovereign states. There is always a measure of natural balance of power in life, but the " balance of power " theory goes beyond this natural adjustment between all the forces of life. Moreover, it presupposed a second principle, that of national sovereignty. Logically the two principles are contradictory ; only a powerful belief in pre-established harmony could assume their compatibility. This confidence was not wholly misplaced. As the frontier situation in America was the most favourable condition for liberal democracy, so the economic world-frontier situation of early capitalism was the most favourable condition for the balance of power. In a world with practically infinite spaces for external development and equally infinite possibilities for internal development, conflicts between states, though not avoidable, were not fatal in their consequences. Always some nations were not involved ; wars between nations did not become global wars. World was still an idea but not yet a reality.

Today, *world* is a reality. The conflict between absolute national sovereignty and automatic harmony expressed through the balance of power has become manifest. The more internal and external extension by individual nations was blocked by world competition and the industrial development of backward and subject peoples, the sharper and more sanguine became international conflicts. The formation of the *League of Nations* was a recognition of the breakdown of natural harmonies in international relations. But the League, like state interference in economics and bureaucracy in domestic politics, was a half-way measure. It sought to limit sovereignty, but on the basis of the recognition of sovereignty. The League members retained final sovereign rights. Thus it saved the principle of sovereignty as state-interference saved the principle of monopolistic production. And in similar fashion, it evoked resentment in some sovereign nations guaranteed by it, just as state-interference evoked resentment in monopolist capitalists who were maintained by it.

In comparison with the ambiguity of the League of Nations, *Fascism* attempted a radical solution. It wiped out lesser sovereign states and created unity by conquest and economic consolidation. This destruction of sovereignty and balance of power by military occupation may produce a trend back to absolute sovereignty. Hate of the conquerors by the subjugated peoples is already leading to an increase of national fanaticism and self-reliance. It is ominous that in Asia enmity toward the white race drives in the same direction, toward intensified nationalism and exaggerated claims of absolute sovereignty. In the meantime, the necessity of achieving world unity tempts the victor nations to establish a centralized system of world domination under their control, but raises the question whether one group of nations can establish unity in the world without destroying creative freedom throughout the world. In still other quarters, there are efforts to find a " *third way* " in terms of " federation."

To the latter *Christianity* may lend its support as it must support the third way in economics and domestic politics. But Christianity must raise the question : What is the realistic basis of federation ? Without a common ground in the substance of social life, federation cannot survive. Such a unifying basis may be found in the first instance in the obvious economic interdependence of all the nations. Indeed, the problem of international relations is much more likely to be solved by this emphasis than by a direct attack upon national prejudices and loyalties which may well be aggravated rather than allayed by the War. But beyond the undermining of absolute sovereignty through stressing the economic unity of mankind, Christianity must stress the necessity of a common spirit within each federation of nations.

D

IV. THE PRESENT WORLD SITUATION IN THE
INTELLECTUAL REALM

IN the *first period* of modern history, the realm of
knowledge and philosophy was the most important for
discerning the deeper character of the age.   Here
belief in autonomous reason declared and justified
itself to the mind of man.   Reason was conceived as
the organ of truth, in philosophy as well as in science,
in the humanities as well as in psychology and sociology.
The development of reason as the quest for truth was
identified with the development of humanity.   If every
individual surrenders himself to the search for knowledge, truth will be discovered, and a " natural system "
of thought and action will be established.   Truth was
conceived as the truth about life as a whole, embracing
politics, ethics, æsthetics, religion.   Although mathematics furnished a pattern of method, all realms of
being and meaning were to be included in the construction of the " natural system of thought and life."
The eighteenth century delighted to call itself the
" philosophical century," not because it was productive
of great systems but because it sought to bring every
aspect of life within the sway of philosophy, in both
theory and practice.   Thus reason in the eighteenth
century was revolutionary reason.   It was not interested
in describing what is merely because it is, but because
it supplies materials for the reconstruction of society
in conformity to what is natural and reasonable.

Very different was the outlook of the *nineteenth century*.
The gargantuan mechanism of an industrial civilization
was swelling to the height of its power and bringing
every aspect of thought as well as life under its sway,
thus radically transforming the guiding principles of
the human mind as well as the actual conditions of
human existence.   Reacting against the revolutionary

rationalism of the eighteenth century, the spirit of the
times became sceptical, positivistic and conservative in
every respect with the single exception of technical
science.   The natural sciences furnished the pattern
for all knowledge, and also for practical life and religion.
Science itself became positivistic : reality must simply
be accepted as it is ; no rational criticism of it is
permissible.   The so-called " fact " and its adoration
replaced the " meaning " and its interpretation.
Statistics replaced norms. Material replaced structure.
Logical possibilities replaced existential experience.
The quest for truth became a method of foreseeing
the future instead of creating it.   Rational truth was
replaced by instincts and pragmatic beliefs. And the
instincts and beliefs were those of the ruling classes and
their conventions.   Philosophy was largely restricted
to epistemology.   It became the servant of technical
progress, its scientific foundations and its economic
control. Following the breakdown of belief in rational
truth as the determining factor in life, " technical
reason "—not aspiring to provide truth but merely to
furnish means toward the realization of ends determined
by instincts and will—became decisive throughout the
world as far as the dominance of Western influences
reaches.

The general trend in the *first two periods* of the modern
development is clearly reflected in men's attempts to
interpret themselves. It is the story of man's estrange-
ment from himself and of his efforts to return to himself.
After he had divided human nature into two distinct
realities after the manner of Descartes—the " thinking
self" and the " extended self"—he detached his
thought from each of these realities and made each
of them objects alongside other objects, to be analyzed
and subjected to general laws as he might analyze
and classify a stone or an amœba.   His physical

mechanism, without spontaneity, and his psychological mechanism, without freedom, were separated from each other and then, one after the other, treated as elements in the universal mechanism of nature, in terms either of physical mechanics or of mechanistic psychology or of a metaphysical mechanism assumed to underlie both. In this fashion, the living unity of all human existence became lost in the process of man's self-interpretation. Man had become a part of the abstract mechanism he himself had created for purposes of control. He had become a part of the machine into which he had transformed himself and his world in both theory and practice. In order to establish control of reality for mechanical ends, man had lost himself. This self-estrangement was the price he had to pay modern science and economy.

To be sure, there were always reactions against the dominant tendency—old feudal and new mass revolts against the practical dehumanization of life, old idealistic and new vitalistic protests against the loss of spontaneity, of creativity, of concreteness in conceptions of man's being and of reality generally. But these reactions were suppressed as long as the bourgeois spirit was mounting in power and the contradictions of bourgeois civilization were not yet apparent. The tremendous success of natural and technical sciences doomed every theoretical protest against their universal applicability to futility.

As we might expect, it was in the *æsthetic realm* that the same all-embracing tendencies found most sensitive and extreme manifestation. And, in accordance with a principle we noted earlier, it was in the field of the arts that the reaction from the dominance of a technical civilization and its consequences for personality first became evident.

Naturalism in literature and art accompanied the triumph of the mechanistic economy of large-scale production and its theoretical counterpart, the mechanization of all reality. Aesthetic naturalism, like scientific naturalism, started with the realm of objective reality. *Realism* was the depiction in word and colour of a world under the domination of mechanism, the "second nature." But it revealed both the enmity between man and his creation and the gulf between man and man in the prevailing society. Inevitably there was a strong reaction against realism. It threatened the society which for decades had sought to cover its brutal reality with idealistic pretensions. Thus naturalism retreated into the realm of the subjective, trying to describe the impression reality makes upon the sensual subject. *Impressionism* is subjective naturalism which uses objective reality with all its distortions and horrors as material for æsthetic intuition. It is a method of escape, available only to those belonging directly or indirectly to the ruling groups, into a sphere of *l'art pour l'art* in which æsthetics becomes an end in itself and man's alienation from himself is forgotten through pure æsthetic enjoyment. Thus æsthetic naturalism had a double significance. On the one hand, it was an expression of the general development of the second period, supporting its dominant trend toward a mechanized world. On the other hand, it was also a disclosure of the self-alienation of man in this period, and thus has contributed to the revolutionary reactions of the succeeding epoch.

Naturalism in its two forms was the great creative style of nineteenth-century art and literature. To be sure, it was not the only one. Romantic and classical opposition were always present since bourgeois society was never all-embracing. But only those æsthetic works showed creativity and progress which either were in harmony with the general trend toward a mechanized naturalism or anticipated revolutionary opposition to it. Idealism in art and philosophy was cultivated by the middle-class creators of the " second nature " as a veil over the naturalistic face of Leviathan. When the veil was torn away by the contradictions of history and the rapid proletarianization of this group, they often became principal supporters of Fascism.

The development from the second to the *third period* is revealed in the realm of art by expressionism and surrealism. It is worthy of note that the artists and writers of the early twentieth century showed an almost prophetic sensitivity to the catastrophes soon to come. They turned away from naturalism in both its forms, either in the more mystical manner of expressionism or in the more demonic-fantastic fashion of surrealism. *Expressionism* has been well characterized as the warning of the earthquake which was approaching. In *surrealism*, the mechanisms of bourgeois society are used and cut into fragments at the same time, the real world disappears and objectivity is transformed into a phantasmagoria constructed out of pieces and fragments of the bourgeois reality. A panic-driven humanity reveals the doom of its world in its artistic and poetic creations.

Since the close of the nineteenth century, the breakdown of mechanistic naturalism in all fields of knowledge has become apparent. History, psychology, biology, physics and even mathematics entered a period of crisis with respect to their true foundations, their interrelations, and their meaning for life. A unifying truth was sought, a truth not merely theoretical but also practical. *Philosophy* itself helped to prepare the new situation. Against the imperious reign of technical reason yielding the detached impersonal knowledge of mechanistic naturalism, there arose the demand for knowledge concerned with life in which the very existence of the knower himself is involved. " *Existential truth* " was the new goal. A truth which concerns us as living, deciding men has a character quite different from the truth which reason, whether humanistic reason or technical reason, was supposed to provide. It is not general truth to be accepted by everyone on the basis of his rational nature. It cannot be gained by detached analysis and verifiable hypothesis. It is particular truth claiming validity on the basis of its adequacy to the concrete situation. Existential truth in its many forms has one common trait : it has no criterion beyond fruitfulness for life. The dismissal of reason as guide to truth is the surrender of any objective standard of truth. Consequently the only basis of decision between contradictory claims to represent concrete truth is a pragmatic test : the power of an " existential truth " to make itself universal, if need be by force. Thus political power could become the standard of possession of truth.

Truth which concerns life, it was claimed, must originate in life. But, whose life ? The " philosophies of existence " are as different from each other as the experiences out of which the various philosophers of existence interpret reality. It can be the ethical existence of the anxious and lonely individual concerned about eternity, as with Kierkegaard. It can be the revolutionary existence of the disinherited proletariat concerned about its future, as with Marx. It can be the existence of the dominating aristocracy concerned about its power over life, as with Nietzsche. It can be the existence of the vital intuitionist concerned about the fulness of experience, as with Bergson. It can be the existence of the experimenting pragmatist, as with James. It can be the faithful existence of the religious activist, as with apostles of the Social Gospel. In each of these definitions of existence, truth has a different content ; but in each of them truth is a matter of fate and decision, not of detached observation or of ultimate rational principles. Nevertheless, it is claimed to be *truth*, possessing universal validity though not general necessity. It is supposed to be verifiable by subsequent experience, although not in the fashion of scientific experimentation.

The issue of existential truth has arisen and cannot be silenced. But it is ambiguous : On the one hand, it represents a protest against the mechanism of production to which reason as a principle of truth has been surrendered. On the other hand, through existential truth the mechanism, the " second nature," is greatly strengthened. For existential truth also surrenders reason and uses only technical rationality for its non-rational purposes. It dissolves the criterion of truth and with it the safeguard against irrational forces.

Truth in this sense concerns human existence as such, and not specialized knowledge except in so far as the latter is dependent, directly or indirectly, upon decision about the nature and meaning of human existence. " Existential truth " need not interfere with methods of empirical research ; it does interfere with the interpretation of the meaning of such research and its results. It does interfere with the foundations of knowledge, with man's understanding of himself and his situation in the world.

The issue, therefore, concerns not only philosophy but also all realms of knowledge. The steady progress of knowledge in the special sciences is not questioned, but their relation to other sciences, to truth as such, to the totality of life, to the meaning of existence. It is the issue of the right relation between empirical and existential knowledge.

In practice, it is always difficult to draw a clear line between empirical and existential knowledge. The totalitarian systems have drawn a boundary in such fashion that everything with direct bearing upon technical processes and therefore on the power it supplies over nature and man is left outside of the question of existence. Technical science is not interfered with. Its task is merely to produce tools by which "existential truths" may be carried into reality. All other realms of life have lost their autonomy and are required to express the chosen existential truth. Thus, in the third period of modern society, technical reason is employed to execute the commands of an existential decision above which there is no rational criterion. The vitalistic interpretation with its irrationalism is radically opposed to the revolutionary interpretation with its cold use of reason for chosen ends—a basic contrast between Fascism and Communism. But in both cases, the idea of truth is grounded in a particular type of human existence which claims to have discovered an existential truth which is at the same time universal.

The abuses of existential thinking and the self-estranged position of reason demand an answer in which existential truth and ultimate truth are united. A very similar demand faced *Christianity* in its earliest period when Greek rationality, empty of all vitality and relevance for life, met a new existential truth springing from the experience and faith of the young Christian community. At this critical moment in its history, Christianity found an answer in its Logos Doctrine. It pointed to a concrete event which it passionately proclaimed as both existential and universal truth for every man—the specific and concrete embodiment of the ultimate divine reason. "Jesus the Christ is the Logos." In this brief formula, early Christianity united, at least in principle, existential and rational truth.

The present world situation puts an essentially parallel problem before Christianity. It must give essentially the same answer though in different terms and with different intellectual tools. Above all,

Christianity must seek to develop the Church toward
an inclusive reality which unites different existential
interpretations as far as they are compatible with each
other and with Christian principles. The more the
Church succeeds in this, the more readily can it receive
rational truth as an inherent part of Christian faith.
If rational truth, with its contributions to the different
realms of knowledge, is excluded, Christian faith
necessarily becomes sectarian and exclusive. If existential truth with its practical bearing on religious and
ethical activity is excluded, Christian faith becomes
relativistic and sterile. Only by a proper union of the
two can the intellectual needs of our present world
situation be met.

V.   CHRISTIANITY IN THE PRESENT WORLD SITUATION

CHRISTIANITY is a faith and a movement far older than
bourgeois society. In its nineteen centuries of history,
it has had to come to terms with the most diverse
cultures and philosophies. Inevitably it has adapted
itself to the development of modern civilization in its
three successive phases. But the relation of Christianity
to any culture can never be adequately interpreted
merely in terms of adaptation. By the very nature of
its message, it must seek to transcend every particular
historical situation, and history demonstrates that the
Church has in fact succeeded always in maintaining
some measure of independence. Therefore, the rôle
of Christianity today can be seen as one of both adaptation to, and transcendence over, the present world
situation.

In so far as Christianity has adjusted itself to the
character of modern society, it is able to bring only a
very incomplete answer to its problems, for Christianity,
as it has been drawn into the destructive contradictions

of the present stage of history, is itself a part of the problem. In some measure this is true of the Church in every age. But it is especially important in the present period because the latter by nature has less affinity to a Christian order of life than former periods.

Indeed, in the later Middle Ages and at the Reformation, religion itself helped to prepare the soil for the growth of autonomy in all realms of life. Religion revolted against the totalitarian control exercised by the Roman Church. Through the pre-Reformation and Reformation attacks upon Catholic authoritarianism, religion paved the way for the auto-nomous national state and the independence of science, economics and the arts. Religion liberated personality and community from hierarchical control. Above all, religion freed itself from ecclesiastical bondage.

But in so doing, religion helped to create alongside itself a secular sphere which step by step invaded and mastered the religious sphere. Thus religion itself became secularized and was drawn into the conflicts and contradictions of the new society. This process can be clearly discerned in every major aspect of that society.

The growth of secular *arts* independent of the Church not only impoverished the religious arts but secularized them. They became secular arts with a religious content instead of religious art with a universal content. We have noted this transformation in the development from Giotto through Titian and Rembrandt to the various schools of contemporary painting. Indeed from a religious perspective, expressionism may be interpreted as an attempt toward a new religious style and a new fusion of religion and art. The failure of this attempt proves that contemporary life cannot be expressed in a genuine religious style. Christianity cannot change this situation merely by ritual reforms however useful they may be.

A new unity of cult and art is necessary and this can be effected only if the present separation of the secular realm from the religious realm is overcome. Religious art presupposes a religious reality embodying a transcendent source and a spiritual centre. The totalitarian attempts to create such a reality on a limited and immanent basis have produced only a few fragments of quasi-religious art. Their sterility in this respect proves that they lack any ultimate and universal significance. But at least they have sensed the problem, while the problem of religious art as the expression of true religious reality has not yet been widely recognized within the Christian Churches.

The emergence of autonomous *personalities* and *communities* has virtually destroyed true religious personality and community.

With the supremacy of autonomous reason, the transcendent centre of *personal life* was destroyed and personality was broken into divergent elements, the unity of which was partially maintained by the continuing hold of traditional beliefs or by conventional and technical demands. Within the religious sphere, personality fought a desperate struggle against dissolution. From Pascal's protests against the Cartesian mechanization of human existence to Kierkegaard's passionate affirmation of the " existential personality," the person in the crisis of decision about his eternal destiny, and Dostoievski's vivid contrast between Jesus' personal confrontation with God and the Inquisitor's secular arrogance, the battle to maintain true religious personality continued. But, for the most part, theology did not follow these prophets because its effort was mainly one of negative resistance. In this attempt some present-day theology has returned to antiquated forms of orthodoxy and produced a fighting type of religious personality great in its negations but weak in its affirmations. For example, Barth sought to save Christian personality from both secular disintegration and totalitarian mechanization, but did not produce a new type of personal life. His movement did not attempt to master the new Leviathan but rather retired before it, and thus left the field to the fanatical dynamics of the totalitarian " impersonal personality."

Religious community, prepared by the lay movements of the later Middle Ages and carried to fulfilment by the Reformation and Sectarianism, was another victim of the development. Religious community must be grounded upon objective beliefs and sacraments. It can be created for a short time by collective enthusiasm but it cannot endure in this form. It requires " objectivity." And, since the rise of autonomous reason, there was no universally potent objectivity except the mechanical objectivity of a technical process. Therefore religious community was largely destroyed, as was religious personality, because a determining spiritual centre was lacking. There was, and still is, a religiously coloured society, but there is no true religious community. The general religious background of society resists the destructive influence of naturalism as long as the background persists. But when it has exhausted itself, the way is open for new totalitarian systems. Totalitarianism, especially in its early phases, produced fighting groups with an absolute faith, an unconditional devotion and a dominating spiritual centre. They are neither religious communities nor religious societies, but fanatical orders with quasi-religious features in which both personality and community are swallowed up.

Especially clear and important is the situation in the *intellectual realm*. The triumph of autonomous knowledge, particularly in the natural sciences, has pushed aside religious knowledge. Either it is repudiated altogether or it is relegated to a corner, or it is transformed by secular interpretations. The last fate is the most disastrous just because it appears to preserve the whole body of Christian truth. In reality it alters the meaning of all beliefs. It makes them a phase of secular knowledge, knowledge which deals only with *some* objects within the whole of reality or with *some* subjective processes mainly in the sphere of feeling. Religious ideas are drawn down to the level of physical or psychological objects. God comes to be thought of as one being alongside other beings, even though the highest. Christ is regarded merely as an historical person whose character and very existence are at the mercy of the conclusions of historical research, very much as God's existence and nature are matters of scientific research or of human value-judgments. Faith becomes one emotion among others, or a lower level of cognitive apprehension ; it conveys probability but not certainty ; its objects may exist or they may not. These transmutations bring religious knowledge into subjection to rational knowledge, and thus destroy its ultimate character. Oscillating between a doubtful objectivity and an unsubstantiated subjectivity, religious knowledge loses its authority. No longer does it express the presence in every reality of the transcendent source of being and meaning ; rather it deals with particular realities, the existence and nature of which are matters either of argument or of irrational belief. But neither the way of argument nor the irrational way of vindicating religious knowledge is able to shake the grip of technical rationality, the former because it remains within the presuppositions of technical reason, the latter because irrationalism is only a negative denial of a false rationalism and is therefore unable to create anything new.

It is a well-known fact that this process of seculari-

zation has affected all of the great religions. Inasmuch
as the influence of Western civilization has penetrated
most sections of the world, religious faith has lost its
power and the danger of a naturalistic quasi-theology
threatens all nations. The absence of a Christian
theology able to express an ultimate reality and spiritual
centre in terms of religious belief has produced scepticism
and cynicism regarding all questions of ultimate concern.

Totalitarianism has sensed this situation, and has
formulated doctrines and symbols supposed to express
an ultimate reality. It has tried to indoctrinate its
followers with an " existential truth." But this ultimate
is not truly ultimate because it does not transcend
relative interests and concerns. It tries to invest a
particular loyalty with unconditional validity. On the
one hand, the totalitarian " theologies " reveal the
final result of the discredit of genuine religious truth
by technical rationality. On the other hand, they
disclose the powerful desire to break through this
situation to new ultimate beliefs and loyalties.

The fate of religious knowledge is symptomatic of
the fate of the *Churches*. The Christian Church should
furnish the answers thrust forth by the present situation
in the economic, political and international orders.
But the Churches largely lack that power because they
themselves have become instruments of state, nation
and economy. After the shattering of the authoritarian
control of Roman Catholicism, national Churches
replaced the one Church. They were supported either
by the state or by the dominant groups in society—
the former predominantly in Europe, the latter especially
in America. In both situations, the Churches largely
surrendered their critical freedom. They tended to
become agencies of either the state or the ruling classes.
Therefore they were unable to conquer the Leviathan
of modern industry, or the liberal dissolution of com-

munity, or the nationalistic disruption of the world. In large measure, they became social agencies for the safeguarding of accepted moral standards. In this fashion, their influence was to support the governing classes and the existing social order, even when criticizing them within the general presuppositions of bourgeois culture. Only prophetic individuals and revolutionary groups attacked the system as such ; the official Churches did not follow. The latter exposed the evils of a class society ; they sought to transcend the national divisions of mankind ; they struggled against the disintegration of liberal individualism. But they did not recognize or understand the deeper nature of the system which they tried to improve.

Inevitably, the totalitarian attack on the system became an attack on the Churches. Indeed, the totalitarian movements put themselves in the place of the Church ; they cannot be rightly understood apart from their semi-ecclesiastical pretensions. Since they offer an all-controlling idea, however demonic it may be, they are in fact serious competitors of the Church. Their attacks on the Christian Churches are thoroughly consistent. They can never tolerate a Church with an absolute claim in competition with their own.

The problem for the Church implicit in this situation is tremendous, especially for the Protestant Churches, and most especially for liberal Protestantism. Protestant orthodoxy can hold aloof from the present world situation, at least to a considerable extent. Roman Catholicism can look forward to the moment when anti-Christian totalitarianism will be replaced by a revived Catholic totalitarianism. Liberal Protestantism can go neither way. It must, however, solve the problem of its relation to the present stage of civilization. It must not return to a position of servant to a social and cultural system whose contradictions have now become manifest. On the other hand it must not follow the totalitarian way in either its pagan or its Catholic form. Only if liberal Protestantism becomes truly " Catholic " can it meet the needs of the hour.

Christianity has not only adapted itself to the contemporary world in its dominant aspects. In many respects and to varying degrees, Christianity has transcended modern culture. It has attempted to preserve its authentic message despite all ecclesiastical and secular distortions. Christianity is not only a part of the contemporary world ; it is also a protest against it and an effort to transform it by the power of Christian faith. This is true in both the intellectual and the practical realms, with respect to both belief and life.

First of all, it must be emphasized that Christianity has accepted the reign of reason not only as a factor in the secular world to which it must seek adjustment, but also as an agency for its own regeneration. The acceptance and employment of reason as the principle of truth has dissolved certain orthodox " stumbling-blocks " which had not been touched by the Reformation but rather had been more firmly anchored by the scholastic dogmatism into which Reformation thought hardened. Thus reason has enabled Christian theology to face fresh questions and seek new answers in the light of contemporary insights and problems. Historical criticism of the Bible has liberated Christian truth from legendary, superstitious and mythical elements in the historic tradition. The honest radicalism of this work of Christian self-criticism is something new in Church history and brought values never before recognized or accepted. Without it, Christianity could not have confronted the modern mind and made its message intelligible and relevant to that mind. Much the same

E

may be said of more recent inquiries into the psychological and sociological roots and processes of Christian thought and action.

All this, however, would not have sufficed to protect Christian truth from complete adaptation to the prevailing intellectual milieu. The Christian message itself had to be borne through the high tide of technical rationality. This has been done in three principal alternative ways which we may call the " preserving," the " mediating " and the " dialectical " types. Each type has many varieties. The *first* is represented by *traditional theology* in either strictly orthodox and fundamentalist form or in the form of moderate adaptation to the new influences, adaptation of structure but not of matter. It is due to this type of Christian interpretation that the treasures of the past have been preserved through a period when for many there was no possible way of comprehending them. The *second* type is represented by the so-called *school of mediation* from Schleiermacher, Hegel and Ritschl through liberal theology to certain current formulations of ecumenical theology. These are distinguished from humanism by their refusal to adapt Christianity entirely to the demands of current vogues. They are distinguished from orthodoxy by their readiness to re-examine all theological issues in the light of the questions of our day. It is due to this type of Christian reinterpretation that theology has continued a living power in the Church and the world. The *third* type is represented by Kierkegaard and his followers who, though themselves shaped by the modern world, are aware of the dangers of adaptation and mediation. The *dialectical approach* rejects the otherworldliness through which the first type seeks to preserve the Christian tradition. It breaks the protecting shell to reveal the relevance of its content to our time. But it does not intercept this content through the ideas of our period ; thus it differs from the second type.

Rather, it relates these to each other in radical criticism. In this sense it is dialectical. It delights to declare ' No " and " Yes " in the same breath. It is due to his type of Christian interpretation that both the dangers of all adaptations to current thought and also the riches and profundities of tradition have again become visible within the Churches. But the danger of the dialectical method has also appeared. When his type of theological thinking tried to become constructive, it simply relapsed into the mere reiteration of tradition. It became " Neo-Orthodoxy."

Not only in the theoretical but also in the practical realm, Christianity has used reason as an instrument of self-regeneration. Reason has completed the religious emancipation of the layman which had been begun by the Reformation but had been halted among the orthodox Protestant Churches. Following the abolition of the priest's rule, it has broken the minister's rule. The Enlightenment was in certain respects a Protestant lay movement. As such it produced new ideals of personality and community. In many parts of the world it destroyed the patriarchal form of community with all its implications for sex relations, family and workshop. Reason has accomplished much the same emancipation for Christian personality. It has opened it to receive the riches of humanism. It has released the suppressed levels of personal life. It has freed the individual from cruel religious absolutism.

However, Christianity would have been drawn wholly within bourgeois society if it had only used and had not also transcended reason in its practical application. Christian faith had to maintain true Christian life over against the demonic powers of the modern world. This, likewise, was accomplished in three alternative ways, analogous to the three types of theological reinterpretation—the *pietistic* or evangelical, the *ethical* and the *paradoxical* types. *Pietism* in all its varieties has preserved the warmth, intensity and creative power of personal relation to God. It has poured forth spiritual vitality in many directions. It is due to the evangelical tradition that elements of early Christian enthusiasm have never been wholly absent in the Churches of the modern period. The *ethical type*, corresponding to the mediating school in theology, is the most influential in contemporary Christianity. It is not mere morals, as the mediating theology is not mere humanism. In it personal religion and ethical concern are so joined that religion is measured by ethical fruits and the ethical life receives its impulse from religion. It is due to this type of practical Christianity that the latter was able to penetrate different areas of cultural life and for a long time guard modern society from complete relapse into nationalistic paganism. But the inadequacies of the merely ethical form of Christian life became so obvious that a third type arose, corresponding to the dialectical school of theology. The *paradoxical* (or, in Kierkegaard's phrase, the " existential ") *type* transcends both the ethical and the pietistic types. It makes religion the measure of ethics, rather than the reverse, stressing the paradoxical character of all individual Christian existence, denied and affirmed by God at the same time. For the same reason, it transcends the pietistic type which is more interested in intensity of religious experience than in the paradoxical action of God.

Through this resistance of Christianity, both theoretical and practical, against the complete domination of technical reason and technical economy over human life, the Church has succeeded in maintaining an authentic spirituality and transcendence. Despite its partial secularization, the Church has profoundly influenced " Christian " nations and secular culture.

Its very existence was and is a signpost pointing beyond the mechanism created by man's technical skill and now turned against man's freedom and fulfilment. Through preaching, education and action, the Churches have exerted a largely subconscious effect upon both masses and individuals. This often unrecognized influence became strikingly visible in the resistance of the Christian masses to the attempts by pagan totalitarianisms to replace Christianity by tribal cults. Moreover, despite the adaptation of the Churches to modern society, they have produced individuals who recognized, exposed and attacked the system and all Christian subservience to it. The deeper meaning of the present world situation is not unknown to many individuals and groups within the Churches. Indeed, against the nationalistic opposition to the religious and cultural unification of mankind, the Christian Churches have created the Ecumenical Movement uniting Christians of all countries, Christian and non-Christian, enslaved and free. This Movement is the only world unity left in the present demonic disruption of humanity.

VI.   GUIDEPOSTS FOR THE CHRISTIAN ANSWER

IT is not within the province of this chapter to attempt the Christian answer to the questions posed by an analysis of the present world situation. However, certain points which must guide the answer may be indicated.

1. One thing is certain : The Christian message to the contemporary world will be a true, convincing and transforming message only in so far as it is born out of the depths of our present historical situation. No single thinker or theological movement can plumb the depths of the *world* situation. No merely theoretical group and no merely practical group, no one in

America or Russia or China or Europe alone, can claim to comprehend the depths of the present *world* situation. These depths are not simply the depths of suffering or of profound insight or of proletarian revolution or of personal communion, but something of all of these, and more. The more a Christian group embraces elements from all these different aspects of the present *world*, the more adequately will it comprehend the true questions and formulate right answers. This means that the Christian Church can speak authoritatively and effectively to our world today only as it is truly "ecumenical," that is, universal.

2. Next, the Christian answer must accept the modern development as an historic fact which cannot be evaded or reversed, and which, like every historic destiny, is ambiguous in its meaning and value. Our analysis has dealt primarily with the negative features of modern culture, its contradictions and aberrations which demand answers. The answers themselves must acknowledge and accept the positive contributions of the modern period. Here the principal point is the elevation of reason as the principle of truth above all forms of authoritarianism and obscurantism. This is a truly Christian issue even if it be fought out largely in humanistic terms. Christian faith which proclaims Christ as "Logos" cannot reject reason as the principle of truth and justice. The Christian answer must be framed with full recognition that the gains of the bourgeois period must not be lost from the future of mankind.

3. Furthermore, the Christian message must be illumined by the insight that the tragic self-destruction of our present world is the result not simply of the particular contradictions bred by that world but also of the contradictions which characterize human life

always.   History shows that, over and over again, the
achievements of man, as though by a logic of tragedy,
turn against man himself.   This was true of the great
creative achievements of sacramental faith as well as
of the achievements of technical reason.   Therefore
the Christian message cannot anticipate a future
situation devoid of tragedy even if the demonic forces
in the present situation be conquered.   The authentic
Christian message is never utopian, whether through
belief in progress or through faith in revolution.

4. Again, Christianity does not give its answer in
terms of religious escapism.   Rather it affirms that the
influences of divine grace are never absent from each
historical situation.   It relates them directly or indirectly
to the history of divine revelation and especially its
central reality—Jesus Christ.   It repudiates a tendency
among many people, Christians and humanists, to
withdraw from the struggles of our time.   Christianity
faces the future unafraid.

5. Lastly, the Christian answer must be at the same
time both theoretical and practical.   It will have
reality only if it is the answer in action as well as in
interpretation of men and women deeply involved in
wrestling with the times.   Despite the measure of their
bondage to the present world situation, the Christian
Churches are the historical group through which the
answer must be given.

II

CHRISTIANITY AND ITS SECULAR ALTERNATIVES

Theodore M. Greene

DR. TILLICH has traced the evolution of our modern culture and has listed some of the most urgent questions of our time. He has recorded his conviction that Christianity alone can provide adequate answers to these questions. The other authors of this book share his conviction. He recognizes, however, as do we, that most people today, even in so-called Christian countries, reject or ignore the Christian Gospel, either from conviction after due reflection, or from dogmatic secular complacency, or from sheer indifference and inertia.

Dr. Tillich has also insisted that if the Christian message to the contemporary world is to be convincing and transforming it must plumb the depths of the present world situation, make full use of the contributions of various secular movements, avoid utopianism, and be realistic in both theory and practice. The authors of the chapters which follow agree and have done their best to restate the central Christian affirmations and their social and personal implications in as Christian, realistic and modern a way as possible. We all realize, however, that many professing Christians, both clergy and laity, are unaware of the weaknesses of the Christian Church today and are either unwilling or unable to relate the abiding truths of Christianity specifically to contemporary needs.

In short, Christianity is faced today with a gigantic dual task—that of persuading a sceptical and secular age of the truth and power of the Christian Gospel, and that of revitalizing and reorienting the Christian Church itself. This second task, is, in a sense, more urgent, for if the salt hath lost its savour, wherewith shall it be salted ? Yet Christians are also under a perennial obligation to preach the Christian Gospel to all who will listen. Some perfectionists argue that missionary efforts should be postponed until those who already profess Christianity have transformed the Christian Church into a perfect City of God on earth, just as some isolationists argued before Pearl Harbour that America should not attempt international co-operation until she had solved her own domestic problems. Actually, both efforts must be made simultaneously. The two tasks which confront Christians today are complementary aspects of one and the same millenium-old responsibility—to do whatever lies in man's power to make Christianity as vital a force as possible in the lives of individual men and women and in the customs and institutions of their society.

I.   THREE SECULAR ATTITUDES TOWARD CHRISTIANITY

WHY is Christianity rejected or ignored today by so many people even in " Christian " lands ? Dr. Tillich has outlined an answer to this question in historical terms. We can supplement this answer by examining some familiar contemporary attitudes to religion in general, and to Christianity in particular.

1.   *The Attitude of the Ordinary Man*

A great many people are indifferent to religion today, as they have been in other periods and cultures, partly from lethargy and weariness, and partly from preoccupation with routine responsibilities and pleasures. " Lured by elemental needs," says Mumford, " man tends to rest content with their satisfaction. . . . There

must always be a sufficient margin of time and energy
to carry forward the processes that make life-fulfilment
possible."[1]   The average human being is overwhelmed
by the urgencies and distractions of the passing moment.
Labour for food and shelter, anxiety for even minimal
economic security, family responsibilities, and all the
activities incidental to man's natural desire for social
approval—these, in combination, leave little time,
energy and incentive for cultural self-development or
spiritual endeavour.   When the day's work is done he
craves, above all else, gratification of his physical
appetites, recreation, rest and sleep.

This is not to say that he is really happy in this daily
routine which falls so far short of an ideal human
existence.   He also experiences loneliness and frustration ; he judges the actual in terms of the more ideal,
and condemns himself for his shortcomings and society
for the injustices which help to make him what he is.
He knows what it is to be rebellious, discontented,
perplexed or stoically resigned.   Nor is the common
man, even in our society, incapable of escaping from
the dreary wheel to heights of heroism, self-sacrifice
and dedication to a cause greater than himself.   On
the contrary, he has again and again, in both peace
and war, shown his capacity for ennobling secular and
religious loyalties.   Yet such achievement is exceptional
rather than typical.   For most men it is no more than
what T. S. Eliot calls the " shaft of sunlight " of the
fleeting moment ; relatively few are, as he puts it,
" undefeated because they have at least gone on trying."
The majority of mankind live and die more like animals
than like men, with their imaginations hardly quickened,
their spirits barely awakened, their minds and bodies
almost completely immersed in the humdrum of un-
profitable labour and of recreation that fails to recreate.

Mumford also points out that our technological

---

[1] Lewis Mumford, *The Condition of Man.*   Secker & Warburg.

culture, far from freeing us from these coercions, has tended to intensify them. " The more complicated and costly the physical and social apparatus for ensuring man's survival, the more likely will it smother the purposes for which it humanly exists. That threat was never stronger than it is today ; for the very exquisiteness of our mechanical apparatus, in every department of life, tends to put the non-human process above the human end."[1] We have become progressively enslaved to the machines we have built to serve us, progressively addicted to the satisfactions which a greater mastery of nature affords—satisfactions not necessarily evil in themselves but wholly incapable of giving meaning and purpose to life. We have largely lost the inspirations and loyalties of community life that were available to men in primitive cultures and in more religiously oriented periods of civilisation. Mumford's description of the contemporary scene is hardly an exaggeration.

The period through which we are living presents itself as one of unmitigated confusion and disintegration : a period of paralyzing economic depressions, of unrestrained butcheries and enslavements, and of world-ravaging wars. . . . But behind all these phenomena of physical destruction we can detect an earlier and perhaps more fundamental series of changes : a loss of communion between classes and peoples, a breakdown in stable behaviour, a loss of form and purpose in many of the arts, with a growing emphasis on the accidental and the trivial : in short, the earliest form of this crisis was an internal " schism of the soul " as Toynbee calls it, and a break up of the over-all pattern of meaning.[2]

This situation, which is described by many Christian and secular writers in similar terms, greatly increases

[1] ibid., p. 414.　　　　　[2] ibid., p. 14.

the difficulty of the " common man " in finding, or even making an effort to find, a purpose and meaning in life. A spiritually unified community rooted in religious or even humanistic beliefs could provide him with opportunities and incentives for spiritual endeavour which our society fails, on the whole, to provide. Our Churches, in the several denominations, do something to make good this loss ; labour movements, schools, and various social enterprises offer to some the comradeship and contagion of a common loyalty ; the family still functions as a cohesive and inspiring force, though its contribution is often less than it was in earlier generations. But all these, in combination, do not suffice to impel countless average men and women to escape from the monotonies of a sub-human existence. Theirs is

> Neither plenitude nor vacancy. Only a flicker
> Over the strained time-ridden faces
> Distracted from distraction by distraction
> Filled with fancies and empty of meaning
> Tumid apathy with no concentration
> Men and bits of paper, whirled by the cold wind
> That blows before and after time . . .
> Or as, when an underground train, in the tube, stops
>   too long between stations
> And the conversation rises and slowly fades into silence
> And you see behind every face the mental emptiness
>   deepen
> Leaving only the growing terror of nothing to think
>   about . . .[1]

The Christian Gospel is addressed directly to such unhappy lonely souls. " Come unto me, all ye that labour and are heavy laden, and I will give you rest. Take my yoke upon you, and learn of me ; for I am meek and lowly in heart : and ye shall find rest unto your souls." These words have kindled new hope in

[1] T. S. Eliot, *Four Quartets*, Faber, pp. 6, 14.

simple men and women for twenty centuries. The Gospel has again and again helped them to escape from themselves, from emptiness, frustration and despair into a life of self-respect through love of God and man. These people are not bedevilled by sophisticated doubts or deterred by anti-religious convictions. Theirs is not an intellectual problem ; they cannot be reached by books and arguments. Yet they are hungry, often without knowing it, for what Christianity has to offer. If the Christian Church does not reach them, as it can and should, some great secular movement may well engulf them, perhaps in the near future. Like Communism and Fascism, such a movement is likely to assume a quasi-religious character, challenging their ultimate loyalties and requiring of them complete devotion to a cause greater than themselves. There are many in our society who would welcome such a movement if it satisfied what they conceive to be genuine human needs. Sincere and enlightened Christians would also welcome it in so far as it did, in fact, promote genuine human welfare ; but they must fear it in proportion as it substituted false gods for the true God and rested on an unrealistic and utopian conception of man's ability to save himself entirely by his own efforts.

2. *Naïve and Sophisticated Naturalism*

At the opposite pole from these discouraged common folk is a small band of naturalists whose influence, though considerable in academic circles, is largely limited to the intelligentsia of our bourgeois society. Their attitudes vary all the way from the naïve complacency of a youthful Somerset Maugham, through the relatively restrained and dispassionate assurance of a John Dewey or an Ernest Nagel, to the rhetorical belligerency of a Sidney Hook. These attitudes, and the beliefs which they reflect, deserve consideration.

Somerset Maugham describes his own youthful naturalism as follows :

I was glad to learn that the mind of man (himself the product of natural causes) was a function of the brain subject like the rest of his body to the laws of cause and effect and that these laws were the same as those that governed the movements of star and atom. I exulted at the thought that the universe was no more than a vast machine in which every event was determined by a preceding event so that nothing could be other than it was. These conceptions not only appealed to my dramatic instinct ; they filled me besides with a very delectable sense of liberation. With the ferocity of youth I welcomed the hypothesis of the Survival of the Fittest. It gave me much satisfaction to learn that the earth was a speck of mud whirling round a second-rate star which was gradually cooling ; and that evolution, which had produced man, would by forcing him to adapt himself to his environment deprive him of all the qualities he had acquired but those that were necessary to enable him to combat the increasing cold till at last the planet, an icy cinder, would no longer support even a vestige of life. I believed that we were wretched puppets at the mercy of a ruthless fate ; and that, bound by the inexorable laws of nature, we were doomed to take part in the ceaseless struggle for existence with nothing to look forward to but inevitable defeat. I learnt that men were moved by a savage egoism, that love was only the dirty trick nature played on us to achieve the con-tinuation of the species, and I decided that, whatever aims men set themselves, they were deluded, for it was impossible for them to aim at anything but their own selfish pleasures. When once I happened to do a friend a good turn (for what reasons, since I knew that all our actions were purely selfish, I did not stop to think) and wanting to show his gratitude (which of course he had no business to feel, for my apparent kindness was rigidly determined) he asked me what I would like as a present, I answered without hesitation Herbert Spencer's *First Principles*. I read it with complacency. But I was impatient of Spencer's maudlin belief in progress : the world I knew was going from bad to worse and I was as pleased as Punch at the thought of my remote descendants, having long forgotten art and science and handicraft, cowering skin-clad in caverns as they watched the approach of the cold and eternal night. I was violently pessimistic. All the same, having abundant vitality, I was getting on the whole a lot of fun out of life.[1]

There were many young naturalists of this type, though seldom so exultant, on our college campuses before Pearl Harbour ; a few still remain, and more may be expected during the disillusioning post-war years. Their naturalism, whether exultant or plaintive, is often merely a stage in the healthy adolescent rebellion against parental orthodoxy and the conventions of their childhood environment. This rebellion is not really healthy however, if it is necessitated, as so often happens, by a religious bigotry in the home which makes it well-nigh impossible for them gradually to revise and mature their religious belief and which therefore compels the intelligent and honest boy or girl to choose, in college, between Christian faith and intellectual integrity. Nor is sophomoric naturalism healthy when, as also frequently happens, it is the only reasonably coherent philosophy of life which the boy or girl has ever encountered at home, in school, or in the community. Nor, finally, is there any guarantee that adolescent naturalism will be automatically outgrown ; it often hardens into a dogmatic, uncritical or self-satisfied naturalism or transforms

[1] W. Somerset Maugham, *The Summing Up*. Heinemann. Compare this attitude of cruel exaltation with Bertrand Russell's romantic self-pity in his famous essay, " A Free Man's Worship," or with Henley's similar " Invictus." Young naturalists today would hardly express themselves in this Victorian style, but they exhibit essentially the same attitudes and beliefs.

itself into a world-weary and life-weary scepticism and cynicism.

" A Diary of Evolution in a Small Country Town," written by Jane Mander during the last war,[1] so well expresses this familiar pattern of naïve but tragic frustration that it deserves quotation at length despite the many ways in which it is " dated " :

Age

5–12   Accept Bible as written, God, Christ, and the Angels in toto, Fixed Heaven and Hell, the Good and the Bad.

12–14   Believe Bible " inspired," but not all " literal." Shed Fixed Hell. See Satan as Force of Evil. Doubt Divinity of Christ.

14–16   Read Bible as history and legend. Shed Divinity of Christ, and the Angels. Keep God as Love, Justice, and Father of mankind. Have fixed ideas of Right and Wrong, but become interested in the Bad.

16–18   Browning stage. Frame " God's in His Heaven, All's right with the World." Parade aggressive Optimism. Accept " World as it is." Preach Duty of Cheerfulness, etc. Orthodox as to Poverty and the Working Classes.

18–19   Honest Doubt. Learn Omar Khayyám by heart. Shed Heaven. Question personal God. Put away " God's in His Heaven." More liberal as to sin.

19–22   General mental tangle. Study Theosophy and Reincarnation, Spiritualism and Christian Science. Shed personal God. Call Him Force, the First Cause, the Guiding Principle, Universal Law, etc. Believe in Mind over Matter, and Love as Constructive Force. Shed fixed ideas of Right and Wrong. See Sin as Defective Education. Morality the new religion. Frame Henley's " Invictus." Exalt the Self. Believe in Human Nature. Get first glimmer of Evolution. Hear

---

[1] *The New Republic*, March 25, 1916, pp. 211–12.

vaguely of Socialism. Realize the Brotherhood of man with due regard for Classes and Types.

IN NEW YORK

22–23 Discover Bernard Shaw. Shed everything else.

23–25 Plunge into psychology, biology, history. Doubt everything but scientific facts. Shed God in any form. Learn the Relativity of Truth. Meet socialists. Investigate Sex War and Wage War. Have Temperament. Exalt the Intellect. Despise the Average Person. Put " Invictus " away in a drawer.

25–26 Begin again. The new religion—socialism ; the new god—humanity ; the new Christ—the man, the carpenter ; the new devils—poverty, capitalism ; the new heaven and hell—the earth ; the new Bible—Marx, Wells, the Fabian Society, the Economists ; the new sins—ignorance, indifference ; the new temples—the street corner, the lecture hall ; the new idealism—*liberté, égalité, fraternité* ; the new words, Individualism, Communism, Humanitarianism.

26–28 Preach Radicalism, Anarchism, Agitation and No Compromise. Despise Laws, Ceremonies, Traditions, and Precedents. Believe in Free Love. Exalt Sincerity. Proclaim the Facts of Life. Lose Temperament in the flurry of general destruction. Tolerate all Comrades in the March of Progress. Believe in the People and the Natural Rights of Man.

28–30 Doubt adequacy of Anarchism. Begin to suspect The People. Consider Organization, Co-operation, and Education. Study Unions and Statistics. See need for some Compromise. Shed Anarchism and Agitation.

30–32 Join a union. Believe in the Wage War. Preach Unity and Sacrifice for the Good of All. Lead Strikes.

32–33 Doubt possibility of Unity. Suspect motives of leaders. Question effectiveness of Sacrifice.

F

Hazy as to definition of The Good of All. Lose illusions about the People. See hope in Political Action. Shed Unions and the Working Man.

33–34 Go into politics. Learn the value of Compromise. Suspect the wisdom of Sincerity. Drop Free Love. Uphold Laws and Ceremonies. Hide the Facts of Life. Try Merit and Reason upon the politician. Suspect the power of Merit and Reason. Try Money and Influence upon the politician. Perceive their immediate and decisive effect. Suspect possibility of Democracy as defined by Lincoln. Suspect the politician. Suspect myself. Begin to feel tired.

34–35 Shed politics and the politician. Turn to Social Service. Join four Clubs and three movements. Boost the Feminists and Suffragists. Talk, and listen to talk. Begin to suspect movements. Suspect all Human Nature. Get more tired.

35–36 A great weariness. Sick of Action. Sick of words. Sick of humanity. No illusions left. Shed everything. Do nothing. Turn to art.

36–37 Believe in Art. Recover Temperament, but don't mention it. Fall in love with an artist. Believe in love. Believe in the artist. Get married.

37 Have a child, who will begin it all over again.

The experience of many college teachers in the present war has been a revelation to them of what can be done, under favourable conditions, to correct this youthful naturalism and scepticism. During the spiritually bleak period of Coolidge prosperity it was almost impossible to break through the shell of under-graduate indifference and complacency. Since Pearl Harbour, in contrast, college students have exhibited a keen interest in vital human issues and have eagerly read and discussed, when given the chance, the great documents of our Western tradition. Those who have encountered, with surprise and enthusiasm, the Bible, the Greek tragedians, Plato and Aristotle, St. Francis, St. Augustine and St. Thomas, Luther and Sir Thomas More, Descartes and Pascal, Locke and Voltaire, Mazzini and Jefferson, Huxley, Wordsworth and Marx, Dewey and Reinhold Niebuhr have often discovered for themselves that the Hebrew Prophets and the Christian saints and theologians have had some insights which were more profound than those of equally distinguished secular writers. Not all have emerged from this experience convinced Christians ; many have embraced a humanism of one sort or another, and a few have been converted to some form of naturalism or been confirmed in their earlier naturalistic beliefs. But nearly all have gained from the experience a deeper insight into the central problems of human nature and destiny, a greater respect for honest inquiry and sympathetic understanding of alternative points of view, and, above all, a quickened appreciation for that humility which is equally essential to scientific research, philosophical speculation, and Christian faith.

I am not suggesting that academic study, however serious, can of itself generate a meaningful acceptance of Christianity. Participation in the corporate life of a Christian community and first-hand Christian experience are certainly essential. Many of the younger generation today, however, are initially so ignorant of Christianity or so dogmatically hostile to its institutional expression, that it never occurs to them to find out for themselves what Christianity is and what it has to offer. Though their lives are often empty, they are quite unable to diagnose their own need or discover the ways in which this need might best be satisfied. Their secular dogmatism is largely unconscious, since it reflects the orthodoxy of a secular age. They assume quite uncritically that religious faith is necessarily blind and superstitious, that science is the only road to truth, and that human problems, whether individual or social, can of course be solved, if at all, solely by human effort, intelligence and good will. The " Christianity " they reject, if they bother to reject it at all, is an infantile brand which any informed and mature Christian would repudiate with far greater vehemence. This is the only Christianity they know anything about. Hence the imperative need for initial reading and discussion as informed, sympathetic and honest as possible. Only thus can many of them be brought to the point of being willing to hear and reflect upon the challenge of Christianity to each individual and to our society.

Some recent articles by Professor Hook, Dewey and Nagel[1] give expression to a naturalism which, in contrast, is highly sophisticated and aggressively anti-religious and anti-Christian. Theirs is the familiar eighteenth-century theme that Christianity is essentially obscurantist and escapist, that scientific method, properly conceived, is our only source of knowledge and the only reliable way to solve our social problems, and that the contemporary threat of Christian fanaticism to naturalistic honesty and enlightenment must be actively combated.

" The new failure of nerve in Western civilization," writes Hook, " at bottom betrays . . . the same flight from responsibility, both on the plane of action and on the plane of belief, that drove the ancient world into the shelters of pagan and Christian super-naturalism. . . ." He cites, by way of illustration, " the recrudescence of beliefs in the original depravity of human nature ; . . . the frenzied search for a centre of value that transcends human interests ; . . . posturing about the cultivation of spiritual purity ; . . . a concern with mystery rather than with problems, and the belief that myth and mysteries are modes of

[1] Sidney Hook, " The New Failure of Nerve " ; John Dewey, " Anti-Naturalism In extremis " ; Ernest Nagel, " Malicious Philosophies," in the *Partisan Review*, Jan.-Feb., 1943, pp. 2–57. All quotations are from these articles.

knowledge ; a veritable campaign to 'prove' that without a belief in God and immortality, democracy— or even plain moral decency—cannot be reasonably justified " (pp. 2–3).

Hook's anxiety over the revival of the beliefs he so hates is more reassuring than the common lament that Christianity has lost its vitality.

In the schools, the churches, and in the literary arts, the tom-tom of theology and the bag pipes of transcendental metaphysics are growing more insistent and shrill. We are told that our children cannot be properly educated unless they are inoculated with " proper " religious beliefs ; that theology and meta-physics must be given a dominant place in the curriculum of our universities ; that churchmen should cultivate sacred theology before applying the social gospel ; . . . that what is basically at stake in this war is Christian civilization. . . . *Obscurantism is no longer apologetic ; it has now become precious and wilful* (p. 3).

Hook then proceeds to an analysis of this dangerous religious movement. It expresses, negatively, " a loss of confidence in scientific method," or, more subtly, an acceptance of the validity of science within a restricted sphere but a condemnation of " the pre-tensions of scientific philosophy, naturalism, empiricism, positivism—not to speak of materialism . . ." (p. 4). This negative attitude " is transformed into open hostility whenever some privileged, 'private' truth pleads for exemption from the tests set up to safeguard the intelligence from illusion," as in " the frenzy of Kierkegaard who frankly throws overboard his intelli-gence in order to make those leaps of despairing belief which convert his private devils into transcendent absolutes " (p. 4). " These, bluntly put," Hook con-tinues, " are gateways to intellectual and moral irresponsibility. They lay down roads to a happy land where we can gratify our wishes without risking a veto by stubborn fact " (p. 5). Naturalists, in contrast, are realistic, intelligent and open-minded. " The philosophy of naturalism, which whole-heartedly accepts scientific methods as the only reliable way of reaching truths about man, society, and nature [does not], decree what may or may not exist. . . . It does not rule out on *a priori* grounds the existence of super-natural entities and forces. The existence of God, immortality, disembodied souls or spirits, cosmic purpose or design, as these have customarily been interpreted by the great institutional religions, are denied by naturalists for the same generic reasons that they deny the existence of fairies, elves, leprechauns, and an invisible satellite revolving between the earth and moon. There is no plausible evidence to warrant belief in them or to justify a probable inference on the basis of partial evidence " (p. 7).

A naturalist, Hook continues, would be unfaithful to his own philosophy if he refused to examine the evidence for the validity of other, less orthodox, con-ceptions of God. But, alas, he always finds that the alleged evidence is not evidence at all.

Unfortunately, for all their talk of appeal to experience, direct or indirect, religious experientialists dare not appeal to any experience of sufficiently determinate character to permit of definite tests. . . . The kind of experience to which reference is made is not only unique but uniquely self-authenticating. Those who are not blessed by these experiences are regarded as blind or deaf, and under certain circum-stances, dangerous to the community. But is it not odd that those who worship Zeus on the ground of a unique experience should deny to others the right to worship Odin on the ground of a different unique experience ? (p. 7).

Hook then proceeds to a sweeping attack on all organized Christianity, from the Pope to the humblest Protestant sect. He critizes Reinhold Niebuhr, "a radical and honest intelligence," on the ground that not a single one of his positions on the momentous issues of social and political life is dependent on his theology, and he repudiates the doctrine that modern democracy is derived from the dogma that all men are created by God and equal before Him—a doctrine which he brands as "logically invalid, historically false, and irrelevant to the pressing problems of democratic defence and reconstruction" (p. 24).

This defence of science and naturalism is continued by Dewey and Nagel. Dewey beats the naturalistic tom-tom less noisily than Hook but he is not above accusing his opponents of ignorance of history, complacency, provincialism and rhetorical dogmatism. He objects violently to the "intrinsically sceptical, even cynical and pessimistic, view of human nature [that] is at the bottom of all asseverations that naturalism is destructive of the values associated with democracy, including belief in the dignity of man and the worth of human life," because this view puts "a heavy discount upon resources that are potentially available for betterment of human life" (pp. 32–3). Our troubles are all due to our failure to apply the scientific method to the solution of our social problems. Nagel points out with admirable lucidity various misconceptions of science which Christian theologians, among others, have often uncritically accepted. Yet he too feels impelled, in his defence of naturalism, to resort to the emotive rhetoric which naturalists so heartily, and rightly, condemn in their opponents.[1]

[1] Cf. his reference to the religious ideas which are now being "insolently proclaimed" as panaceas for public and private ills and to the "unique mixture of pontifical dogmatism, oracular wisdom, and condescending obscurantism" of Professors Etienne Gilson and Jacques Maritain (pp. 41, 50). Naturalists seem to find it as hard as the rest of us to practise the unemotional scientific objectivity which they preach.

Before attempting to answer these naturalists we must at least mention a dual tendency in contemporary naturalism which makes it difficult to criticize it fairly. It tends, on the one hand, to be nihilistic in reducing objective values to subjective human preferences and by regarding these preferences as essentially irrational and therefore incapable of reasonable defence. It tends, on the other hand, to be humanistic in recognizing man's distinctive nature and dignity and in attempting to develop his higher potentialities. The former tendency has been dominant in the " naturalism " of our Western tradition ; it achieved its clearest expression in the eighteenth-century materialism of Lamettrie and the evolutionary naturalism of the late nineteenth century. Many writers today, in contrast, call themselves naturalists but conceive of " nature " as including values as well as spatio-temporal events, and of the " natural " as embracing all types of human experience, even the mystical. This " higher " naturalism can be regarded as somewhat akin to the contemporary humanism which is examined in the next section of this chapter. Our immediate concern is with the more belligerent and less generous type of naturalism which is in fact reductionistic and subversive of man's higher aspirations, despite the indignant denial of those who defend this position. It is only this tendency and attitude in Hook, Nagel and Dewey which is here criticized ; in so far as they are humanistically minded, their position is considered in our critique of humanism.

What can a thoughtful and sincere Christian say in answer to these naturalists ? He can re-emphasize the important distinction between scientific inquiry and a naturalistic philosophy superimposed upon it. He can then assert the validity of science within its self-imposed limits and accept the genuine insights of naturalism, while rejecting its claim that it alone does justice to all the facts of human nature and the cosmos. He can welcome wholeheartedly the naturalist's sincere concern for human welfare, approve his emphasis on the continual need for human initiative and the use of human intelligence, and confess with sorrow that official Christianity has indeed too often discouraged such initiative, viewed reason and rationality with unjustified suspicion, and thus delayed the advance of human knowledge and its application to the alleviation of human misery. He can and should confess in deep humility his own provincialism and dogmatism and the many instances of such provincialism and dogmatism in the Christian Church.

But he must also, in honesty, return again and again to the attack upon what he is convinced are the errors of the naturalists. Despite their insistence that they do not destroy human values but rather accept them at their face value for what they are found to be in actual experience, he must continue to point out the nihilistic implications of their basic naturalistic position. When Dewey accepts, for example, the dictum of Hippocrates that " all events are equally sacred and equally natural," how can he so ardently deplore certain events and welcome others ? And when Nagel declares that it is " the height of discourtesy and parochialism to damn a society as immoral simply because its standards of excellence differ from one's own," how can he, in the spirit of naturalistic courtesy and enlightenment, justify a rejection of either Hitlerism or Christianity ? A Christian must continue to point out the arbitrariness of the assertion that science is the only road to truth and that naturalism is the only embracing philosophy which can do full justice to the findings and methods of modern science, for this is as provincial and dogmatic a position as any to be found in the history of the Christian Church. He must, by careful analysis, show what are the limits of science, and how scientific truth can and must be complemented by religious insight.

All this, however, is largely negative and destructive criticism. Can a thoughtful Christian do anything to defend his own positive beliefs, by making available to the naturalist the positive evidence and theological interpretations on which they rest? Here his task is well-nigh hopeless, not because such evidence does not exist or because the Christian interpretation of it is invalid but because of the naturalist's stubborn *a priori* conceptions of what constitutes evidence and valid interpretation, because of his profound misconception of Christianity, and, most of all, because of his almost unshakeable complacent confidence in man's self-sufficiency.

Complacency is the most important factor in this picture because it robs the sophisticated naturalist of all incentive to examine the Christian Gospel with real open-mindedness, and, indeed, actively prevents him from doing so. Hence his inevitably distorted picture of the Christian experience as private, self-authenticating, irrational, irresponsible, unrealistic and escapist. The sincere Christian knows that what he can only call his experience of, or encounter with, God is one which he can and does share with other Christians. He knows that, far from being self-authenticating, it confirms and is confirmed by many of his other experiences, and that the Christian interpretation of this experience, far from being irrational, is the only one that seems to him to make sense. He knows that there is no escaping the Divine righteousness, and that faith in God's love and mercy is in no sense an escape from the sinful finitude of human life or the spiritual laws of the universe. But the naturalist cannot know what the Christian is talking about when he uses such language as this, for he is caught in a vicious circle. His naturalistic dogmas induce in him a complacency which stifles that sense of need which Christians and secularists less dogmatic than himself share. Hence his blindness, reference to which he so much resents, and his inevitable " conclusion " that Christian faith is superstitious moonshine.

" If God had willed," says Pascal, " to overcome the obstinacy of the most hardened, He could have done so by revealing Himself so manifestly to them that they could not have doubted of the truth of His essence. . . . It is not in this manner that He has willed to appear in His advent of mercy . . . in a manner manifestly divine, and completely capable of convincing all men ; but it was also not right that He should come in so hidden a manner that He could not be known by those who should sincerely seek Him. . . . Willing to appear openly to those who seek Him with all their heart, and to be hidden from those who flee from Him with all their heart, He so regulates the knowledge of Himself that He has given signs of Himself, visible to those who seek Him, and not to those who seek Him not. There is enough light for those who only desire to see, and enough obscurity for those who have a contrary disposition."[1]

This statement, which Christians accept as wholly in conformity with their experience and observation, is supplemented by another remark which is equally relevant. " When we wish to correct with advantage, and to show another that he errs, we must notice from what side he views the matter, for on that side it is usually true, and admit that truth to him, but reveal to him the side on which it is false. He is satisfied with that, for he sees that he was not mistaken, and that he only failed to see all sides."[2] The first part of this advice is easier to carry out than the second. What humanistically minded naturalists are most concerned positively to assert and promote—the value

[1] Blaise Pascal, *Pensées*, Everyman Edition, Fragment 430.
[2] *ibid.*, Fragment 9.

of scientific method, as they conceive of it, for the solution of social problems as well as for an understanding and mastery of nature ; the value and dignity of man as well as his kinship to nature ; the importance of alleviating human suffering and promoting human welfare—to all this an informed Christian can heartily subscribe. He can also admit that naturalists are fully justified in repudiating, as do Dewey and Nagel, many unfair criticisms of both science and naturalism, and that they have done Christianity a great service by attacking so sharply many of the weaknesses and perversions of the Christian Church. But how can a dogmatically complacent naturalist be convinced " that he has failed to see all sides " ? Argument is futile which is not rooted in a common sense of need. Demonstration is useless if all the relevant facts are automatically and uncritically given a naturalistic interpretation. " They who have ears to hear, let them hear." These naturalists have no ears to hear and no desire to see anything that would call in question the adequacy of their own philosophy. A reasonable criticism of naturalism and a reasonable exposition and defence of Christianity can have value only for those who are less complacent and more open-minded and open-hearted.

3. *Humanism, Assured or Anxious*

There are in our society today many thoughtful people who are not committed to an anti-Christian metaphysic and who recognize the positive achievements of historical Christianity (while deploring its many failures to live up to its own standards), but who find themselves unable to share in the experiences and beliefs of professing Christians and who believe that the Christian Church has lost its spiritual vitality and its ability to accomplish what it has accomplished in the past. They are all in one sense or another humanists—men and women deeply concerned with human welfare, convinced of man's ability to solve his own individual and social problems, sceptical or incredulous regarding the central tenets of Christianity, eager to work with all men of good will for the improvement of man's lot on earth, but fearful lest this co-operative effort be weakened or jeopardized by Christian dogmas to which they, as non-Christians, cannot subscribe.

It is of the utmost importance that Christians do everything in their power to understand the point of view of these humanists in order to learn from them and in order to do what they can to dispel the doubts which prevent them from embracing Christianity. Some humanists who read these pages may feel a sufficiently acute sense of need and may be sufficiently uninhibited by intellectual preconceptions to desire, without further ado, a restatement of the central Christian affirmations and of their social and personal implications. They should proceed at once to the remaining chapters of this volume. A few may even be able to associate themselves at once with some Christian Community and participate at first hand in the Christian experience. But the majority will probably have misgivings which make it impossible for them to examine or re-examine the Christian faith in Pascal's spirit of eager search, or to participate in Christian worship. It is to them that the following pages are primarily addressed.

A recent article by R. P. Blackmur so well expresses several typical aspects of this widespread humanistic attitude that it deserves quotation at some length:

The challenge of the supernatural revelation is one to which I have nothing to respond with. . . . For most people, the supernatural aspects of the Christian tradition are no longer a matter of secular experience, or of any kind of experience, even inherited experience,

or what is called instinct. No doubt much of the
actual is thereby shut out into unknowable unity or
intolerable chaos ; but it is only the natural that can
touch, or drive, or attract the secular mind ; and we
must work with the experience that we have without
the use of experience to which we cannot pretend. . . .
In a desperate world of nature it seems good to get
rid of the unnecessary despair caused by the effect of
asserted supernatural authority to which there is no
access. . . . Can we not at once begin looking . . .
at the things that do exist and are believed, at anarchy
struggling to order, at order combating anarchy : the
very body of beliefs which if we can see them together
give our culture significance? . . . Can we not then
feel of the past, the Christian past and also the human
past of which the Christian was but one effort at
universal expression, not the weight of its dead
formularies, but its permanence in change, its change
in permanence, its pressing, enveloping life : all in
the life we actually live ? Are we not then strengthened
and convicted by the vital dogma, that, as man has
had the power to create imperfectly both his society
and its death many times in the past, so he has now
the power—if he but musters his intelligence and his
will—to create it imperfectly again out of the needs
and desires, the energies and abilities, the institutions
and the individuals, the good conflicting with the
evil, of existing human life : the only materials man
has ever had, in handling which his skill and wisdom,
his fumbling and folly make the whole sum of
what he has been able to transmit : the human
tradition ? . . . I do not know that the effort to
discover and unite by secular means the common
beliefs of the actual world will succeed ; certainly it
will not succeed permanently or completely ; . . . but
I do know that Eliot's kind of effort [i.e., the Christian
effort] is impossible for many and sterile for most of the
people who will have to make whatever effort is made.[1]

[1] " Mr. Eliot and Notions of Culture," *The Partisan Review*, Summer, 1944
(pp. 302–4) written in answer to T. S. Eliot's " Towards a Definition of Culture "
in the Spring, 1944, issue of the same *Review*.

Note that this position differs significantly from aggressive naturalism in some respects and resembles it in others. Unlike Sidney Hook, for example, Blackmur is agnostic rather than atheistic. He does not categorically deny the existence of God and the supernatural, and he is willing to admit that mere human understanding may well " shut out much of the actual." Nor does he subscribe in naturalistic fashion to the dogma that scientific method is the sole source of knowledge and the only reliable guide to human conduct. Indeed, as a humanist, a poet and a critic, he would repudiate this dogma and insist on the revealing power of the artistic imagination.

His rejection of Christianity is based, accordingly, not on a naturalistic dogma but on his own inability, which he shares with other humanists, to participate in the Christian experience and to accept its " asserted supernatural authority." The implication is that he has honestly tried to do so and failed. His disbelief is not defiant or exultant ; it is necessitated by factors which he cannot control and by secular convictions which he cannot honestly abandon.

His reference to the " dead formularies " of official Christianity indicates a belief on his part that they were once alive, once meaningful expressions of a vital faith, but that they have now ceased to reflect a vital faith, even for many Christians who still formally subscribe to them. Yet he does not admit that this faith was ever valid or true ; rather, he regards Christianity, even in its prime, as merely one among other human efforts to give universal expression to man's common heritage. This is quite consistent on his part, for if Christian belief was ever valid, it should be valid now and therefore acceptable to honest and sensitive men.

His final plea for greater confidence in what man can accomplish on his own initiative, and his appeal to Christians not to impair man's corporate effort to combat the forces of evil by insisting on beliefs which non-Christians cannot accept, is equally reasonable from this point of view. The trouble is that sincere Christians are equally convinced that man cannot save himself solely by his own efforts, that this humanistic optimism, even the qualified optimism of Mr. Blackmur, is utopian, that what the humanists call the "supernatural" does exist, and that the only realistic procedure is to make use of the spiritual, as well as the purely human, resources which are available to man. A primitive savage who had no faith in modern medicine might quite reasonably, from his point of view, urge those in his society who did believe in medicine not to resort to medical practices which he and his friends could not support. But a modern doctor would, in view of his belief in medicine, have to stand his ground and insist that it was the savage, and not he, who was being unrealistic.

In short, the issue between the humanist and the Christian reduces itself to a question of fact. If in fact there is no God, as Christianity conceives of Him, or if God has not revealed Himself to man in countless ways and with unique clarity and power in Christ, or if this God cannot do for men what they are unable to do for themselves—if Christian beliefs are false, Christians are the victims of a tragic illusion and are indeed wasting time and energy on religious activities that should be devoted to wholehearted humanistic endeavour. If, on the other hand, the humanists are wrong and the Christian right, it is the humanists who are victimized by illusion and doomed to ultimate frustration ; it is they who are unrealistic and utopian.

This whole approach, however, involves, from the Christian point of view, a fundamental distortion of the central issue because the problem has been formulated thus far exclusively in terms of how man

can benefit or save himself, either on his own initiative
or with Divine aid. That is, the question is stated
in humanistic or anthropocentric terms. The implication is that, if God exists, His chief function is to help
man realize on earth his secular human hopes and
desires, and that man's sole interest in God is to
receive His aid toward the accomplishment of these
human ends. Christianity, in contrast, is theocentric
in its insistence that man has been created to love
and worship God, that God is not one among other
cosmic forces to be exploited by man for man's benefit,
but that God is the proper object of man's highest
loyalty and devotion. This is precisely the distinction
between primitive magical religions and " high "
religions like Christianity. The essence of magic, as
exemplified in primitive religions, is the attempt of
man to exploit the supernatural for his own advantage
—*do ut abeas, do ut des* : I give, in order that you may
leave me alone, or in order that you may give me
what I want. Here religion is a transaction between
man and the supernatural in which man participates
solely for his own benefit. In its highest expressions
Christianity, in contrast, has always insisted that God
be worshipped for His own sake, and loved for Himself,
without primary concern for the ensuing benefits.

But this, too, distorts the Christian perspective.
For Christianity also insists that man's worship of,
and his communion with, God constitute his own
true destiny and his highest felicity. It does not
deny what God can do for man ; on the contrary, it
insists that God can and will do for those who trust
in Him " more than they can ask or think." Sincere
Christians do not worship God *in order* to attain these
benefits ; yet they acknowledge and accept them
with profound gratitude. Is this a hopeless contradiction ? Man's finest experiences of human love
and friendship offer the closest analogy—only an

G

analogy, it is true, but one which helps to give meaning to the Christian's response to God. Human love at its best is simultaneously unselfish and rewarding. Really to love another person is to love him for himself, without hope or expectation of reward ; yet no human experience, save only man's communion with God, is more profoundly rewarding and enriching. Human love at its best is thus neither egoistic nor purely altruistic. In his love for his fellowman, man realizes himself and fulfils himself as he cannot possibly do in purely self-centred striving. Similarly, the universal testimony of Christian mystics, saints and prophets has been to the supreme beatitude of a whole-hearted love of God for His own sake.

Christians also believe that men can truly love their fellowmen only as a result of loving God with all their hearts. The sequence of the two injunctions in the Great Commandment is not accidental but crucial ; only with God's aid, and through love of Him, can we hope to love our neighbours as ourselves. Here again the issue is ultimately one of fact ; it concerns man's essential nature and the nature of the spiritual laws of the universe. Christianity insists that man's natural egoism is so deep-seated that mere human benevolence, however sincere and strenuous, will not suffice to prevent us from using people as means to our own ends, from hurting those we love, from injuring those we most wish to help. Only with God's help can we escape from a self-seeking concern for ourselves and achieve that complete devotion to the welfare of others which humanists, like Christians, believe to be essential to human welfare. A Christian is thus compelled to believe that humanists themselves can accomplish what they themselves most want to accomplish only through Christian faith and with God's aid. True humanism, they honestly believe, is Christian humanism.

Since Christians sincerely believe all this they cannot,

in honesty, accede to Mr. Blackmur's humanistic plea that they discard their Christian faith in order to co-operate with non-Christians on the basis of a common secular experience. They can, and indeed they should, co-operate with humanists as fully as possible for the realization of all human ends which both consider desirable. These include all alleviation of human suffering, all promotion of peace, order, and justice, all forms of education which free man from the tyranny of ignorance and cultivate his natural sensitivity to human values—in short, all that contributes to human well-being. Christianity is not other-worldly in the sense of being indifferent to man's welfare on earth, nor is it opposed to these cultural values. Its refusal to accept them as constituting the whole of human welfare is not a denial of their positive value ; its insistence that they are subordinate to man's communion with God places them in what, from the Christian point of view, is the only proper context.

Christians can also acknowledge, in all humility, that many men and women today who are not professing Christians exhibit a more truly Christian spirit than do many church-goers. They must, indeed, recognize the many weaknesses of institutional Christianity as well as the actuality and power of what Professor Tillich calls the " latent " Church. They dare never forget that God moves in mysterious ways, and they should never presume to insist dogmatically that He accomplishes His purposes only through certain individuals and institutions. This is the burden of Hebrew prophecy and of the prophetic voices of the Christian era. The Christian Church need not, on that account, be regarded merely as one among other ephemeral human institutions. Christians do believe that it is unique, with a unique function which only it can perform, and that it will continue, however inadequately, to perform this function. But they can and should acknowledge and seek to remedy its failures, and they also can and should acknowledge and welcome all that is being done outside the Church for human welfare.

In short, a Christian and a humanist can hope to co-operate only on the basis of complete frankness and mutual understanding and sympathy. Neither can, in the light of his own convictions, ask the other to be dishonest—to abandon beliefs which he sincerely holds or to subscribe to beliefs which he cannot honestly accept. Both must acknowledge candidly all that separates them, and each must do what he can to make as available as possible to the other those crucial experiences which constitute the empirical basis of his belief. This is the purpose of the present volume ; we are here trying to state once again, in contemporary terms, what we conceive to be the essence of Christian faith, in the hope that our sceptical friends will find it less unreasonable and more compelling than they had supposed.

The remainder of this chapter can most profitably be devoted to a brief consideration of some misconceptions of Christianity and of certain secular dogmas which prevent many humanists from taking Christianity more seriously.

II. THE REASONABLENESS OF CHRISTIANITY

1. *The Supernatural*

NATURALISTS and humanists are about equally critical of the " supernatural." They either insist that they can attach no meaning to this term or else give it a meaning which makes belief in it utterly irrational. It is safe to say that no informed Christians—and few professing Christians are informed—believe in the supernatural which these naturalists and humanists repudiate. What, then, do Christians mean by the supernatural? It is quite easy to give a verbal answer to this question but not at all easy to comprehend its true impact.

By the "natural" Christians mean, first of all, whatever has been created by God and what the Bible refers to as a "creature" or the "creaturely." This includes the physical world and man as a psycho-physical being subject to the laws of the universe. God, as the Creator of this creaturely world, is accordingly conceived of as "supernatural."

But the God of Christianity is not the God of eighteenth-century deism, that is, a God who, having created the world, turns it loose and pays no further attention to it. On the contrary, He is the abiding Ground of all being, the continuing Source of all finite existence, the Sustainer of the world as well as its original Creator. Nor is His relation to the world mechanical or impersonal. He is conceived of as a Person who loves the world with a love which resembles, but infinitely transcends, human love. It is this love which has impelled Him to create man in His own image, that is, with a capacity to respond to His love and to enter into communion with Him.

This interpretation of God's relation to man and of human nature distinguishes man from all other creatures and puts him in a unique relation to the supernatural. He has special God-given endowments and is therefore able, and in duty bound, to respond to the Divine Initiative in trust and gratitude. The term "soul," of which many psychologists today are so contemptuous, signifies precisely this spiritual capacity and obligation. The soul is not an isolated entity in man, what Professor E. D. Holt has called a "stellar point soul," unrelated to man's psycho-physical nature and complex personality. It is the whole of man, as we know him in this life, in his capacity for spiritual aspiration and achievement, for love of God and obedience to Him. This is what the poetic phrase " resurrection of the body " in the Apostles' Creed emphasizes. The immortality of which Christianity assures us is a spiritual achievement of the whole man in this life and of man as a total personality after death. Man thus partakes of the supernatural by being " inspirited " by the Divine Spirit ; he grows in spiritual stature as a son of God by being " possessed " by God. His " soul " is therefore his entire being in its potential and actual orientation to God, his Creator.

To grasp the full Christian meaning of this concept of the supernatural and man's relation to it, we would have to explore the rich Christian concepts of God as a Divine Person, of man as a finite person created " in the image " of God, and of the unique Thou-I relation of God to the human soul. But even on the bases of this brief statement we can ask whether such a concept of the supernatural is either quite meaningless or wholly incredible.

It is meaningless only to those whose initial conception of meaning makes it meaningless. If, for example, only that is meaningful which is ultimately reducible to sensation, or verifiable through sensation, God and the soul are certainly meaningless terms— but so are thought, personality, value and, indeed, everything to which humanists and many naturalists attach supreme importance. Similarly, if only that is meaningful which is completely understood, or even understandable, by the human mind, it follows that what Christians refer to as supernatural is again not meaningful, for Christians are unanimous in believing that man cannot completely fathom God's nature or fully understand the human soul and its ultimate destiny. Yet both naturalists and humanists make use of such concepts as " nature " and " man " without thereby claiming that man does, or perhaps ever will, fully understand the " objects " to which they refer.

It seems clear, then, that the supernatural, as the Christian conceives of it, is not a wholly meaningless concept. If it were, the atheist's disbelief and the agnostic's doubt would be as meaningless as the Christian's faith, for one cannot meaningfully even deny or doubt what is wholly meaningless.

Is, then, the reality of God and the soul necessarily and by definition incredible? Only a secular dogmatist would be so bold as to assert that it is. On what reasonable basis could one possibly be sure that the world of nature comprises the whole of reality, unless one equates " nature " with " reality " by definition, or that man is merely a spatio-temporal being incapable of spirituality unless again one sets dogmatic limits to man's potentialities? It surely does not take very much imagination to conceive of the possibility that reality may have aspects or dimensions which are not evident to sense or even wholly comprehensible by human reason. Pascal's dictum, " Not all that is incomprehensible ceases to exist," would seem to be far more reasonable than the rationalistic dogma that only the rational is real and that the whole of reality is at least theoretically comprehensible by human reason.

The Christian concepts of God and the soul are therefore neither meaningless nor necessarily untrue. This does not suffice, however, to give us any reasonable assurance that the God of Christianity and the human spirit are real. What, then, is the positive basis for the Christian belief in God and the human soul?

2. Revelation

The general Christian answer to this question is that God has revealed Himself to man in many different ways—in the world of nature, in man's basic human experience of being a finite self-transcending creature, in the distinctive religious experiences of mystics, saints, and prophets, and, more particularly, in the individual and corporate experiences recorded in the Bible, culminating in man's encounter with the historical Jesus and continuing in the recorded testimony of the Christian Church. Is there anything initially incredible in this claim?

If the Christian's apprehension of God is true and if in fact He does possess the attributes assigned to Him by Christianity, it is certainly not incredible that He should have revealed Himself to man in various ways, or in distinctive ways to a certain people, or even uniquely in a single historical individual, or with special clarity to the members of a continuing Christian community. What is there in science, history or philosophy to preclude this possibility? The only reasonable response to this claim would seem to be to study the alleged religious experiences and the Christian interpretations of these experiences as open-mindedly as possible, for if the claim has any validity at all it is, indeed, of momentous import to man.

Such a study would make it evident that the religious experience in general, and the Christian experience in particular, is uniformly described by those who have had it as an encounter with a *real* Being whose nature has partially manifested itself in this encounter. What are the criteria of the reality of any " object " of experience? They are, in brief (a) coerciveness, (b) coherence, and (c) publicity.

(a) We accept as " objectively real " whatever, first of all, intrudes itself upon our consciousness with a character of its own which we ourselves cannot change but must accept for what it is. It is the coerciveness of sense experience, for example, which compels us to take this experience seriously as, in some sense, an experience of reality.

(b) But mere coerciveness is not enough, for dreams,

illusions and hallucinations may be coercive and none the less misleading. What is misleading in these cases, however, is not the coercive " given " but the interpretation placed upon it. Only that is accepted by us as objectively real which we can make coherent with some order of reality. Thus, " veridical " (i.e., reliable) sense experiences are judged to be trustworthy clues to what we regard as " real " physical objects, whereas other equally vivid and coercive experiences are called dreams, illusions or hallucinations.

(c) Finally, there is no reason why any given individual should not have a perfectly valid experience of the real which is quite unique, wholly private, and unshared or even unsharable by other men. Indeed, all new discoveries are, at the outset, the private and unique insights of single individuals, and the fact that some of these insights are hard to communicate to others does not in itself invalidate them. None the less, men are not only incorrigibly social ; their knowledge of themselves and their environment is essentially the product of human co-operation and communication. Solitary confinement is the most cruel of all punishments ; the inability to communicate with others and to share one's experiences with others is a recognized cause and criterion of insanity. The first desire of a scientist who believes himself to have made a new discovery is to await the confirmation of other competent scientists. The first impulse of any man who has an unusual experience is to ask someone he trusts, " Do you see, or hear, or feel what I do ? " The third criterion of reality, therefore, which complements the criteria of coerciveness and coherence, is publicity : only that is judged to be undeniably real which others, at least those who are qualified to do so, can also experience and interpret in the same way.

The phrase, "who are qualified to do so," is important

in every type of experience. The negative testimony of the blind and the deaf does not make us distrust the reliability of our senses. The inability of non-scientists to repeat the experiments or to understand the interpretations of modern science does not discredit these experiments or interpretations. The same is true in such realms as technology, law, or art ; in each realm some men are more expert and wise than others. We realize that man's knowledge of reality is always an aristocratic enterprise in which not all men can share equally. Competent scientists, artists, lawyers and engineers speak with an authority which their peers accept on the basis of first-hand verification and which others accept with a humility which is proportionate to their own sense of limitation in the field in question. Authority has, in secular life, a dual meaning ; it signifies, on the one hand, the compulsion to assent which characterizes whatever is, to any given individual, simultaneously coercive, coherent, and sharable ; it signifies, on the other hand, what is more or less blindly accepted at second-hand. A scientist accepts as authoritative in the first sense what he himself has verified and confirmed. The common man accepts the pronouncements of scientists as authoritative in the second sense. He does so, despite the fact that he cannot verify or even understand them, partly because he has indirect evidence, e.g., in the practical applications of science, that these scientists know what they are talking about, and partly because he is convinced that, as a group, they are both honest and able.

The authority of Christian Revelation should be interpreted along these same lines, despite the contrary belief of dogmatic naturalists. In direct proportion as Christians have shared at first-hand in the Christian experience and have thought through the Christian interpretation of this experience, this interpretation is accepted as authoritative in the first sense. The large measure of agreement among the prophets, evangelists and saints of the Hebraic-Christian tradition is impressive. They confirm one another's testimony again and again. They agree that the God whom they claim to have encountered presented Himself coercively to them with a character of His own ; they agree in broad outline in their interpretation of these coercive experiences. In short, their religious experiences, though necessarily private in the sense in which all experiences are private, are sharable, communicable and verifiable. But in religion, as in science, some men are more sensitive, imaginative and informed than others ; Christianity is, in its own way, as " aristocratic " as science. But its " aristocratic " character must be conceived in appropriate terms and not by reference to irrelevant standards. We are here dealing not with a social or intellectual aristocracy but with a spiritual aristocracy—the aristocracy of those, of however humble a social origin, and with however limited scientific or philosophical capacity and training, who possess the humility, the earnestness, the sense of awe, and the capacity for utter devotion to God and man which are simultaneously the condition and the criterion of religious insight.

On the other hand, in proportion as men, both within and outside the Church, are unable to participate in this distinctive experience or to comprehend its Christian interpretation, they must initially either accept or reject the authority of Christian Revelation at second hand.[1] Secularists who reject it simply because it is not reducible to, or verifiable in, purely secular terms do so at their own peril. The simple

[1] The Christian Church at its best has always regarded such second-hand acceptance as a second-best course of action, vastly inferior to acceptance on the basis of understanding and first-hand experience.

Christian is less dogmatic and more humble. He is willing to believe that the Bible is indeed the record of God's revelation to man even though he very inadequately comprehends this revelation. He is willing to credit the testimony of the prophets and saints even though he cannot fully verify this testimony in his own experience and reflection. His acceptance of what Mr. Blackmur calls " asserted " authority, whether Biblical or ecclesiastical or a combination of the two, *is* blind in proportion as it is, for him, merely asserted and not confirmed first-hand experience. Such blind faith is as unsatisfactory, and as hazardous, in religion as elsewhere. But the faith of sincere Christians is never wholly blind ; it is always rooted, to some extent at least, in their personal encounter with the Jesus of history and the spirit of Christ in the Church, and in their own experience of prayer and religious meditation.

God's revelation of Himself to man need not, there-fore, be interpreted superstitiously, though it often has been and still is so interpreted by many Christians. It is not incredible. It has been profoundly meaningful and utterly convincing to the religiously sensitive in the entire Hebraic-Christian tradition, and it has been more or less shared by countless Christians through the centuries of our Christian era.

3. *Reason, Faith, and Dogma*

It can still be asked whether what has just been said about revelation is a fair account of the Christian attitude toward the authority of the Bible and the Church. To answer this question we must first dis-tinguish between the Roman Catholic and the Protestant positions. The former, in general, gives priority to the Church over the Bible in the sense that it regards the Church, and particularly the Pope, as the ultimate interpreter of Scripture, though the

Bible is of course also accepted as the record of God's revelation of Himself to man. The Protestant doctrines of the " priesthood of all believers " and the centrality of the Word make the Bible the Christian's ultimate authority and the individual Christian ultimately responsible for his interpretation of it. The fear that such reliance on each individual Christian would lead to disagreements and heresy has led Protestant fundamentalists to try to exclude the factor of individual interpretation by insisting on the literal truth of every word in the Bible. It is a similar fear that has led Roman Catholics to attribute absolute authority to the Church's interpretation of Christian doctrine.

Both these positions represent, in effect, a determination to safeguard the authority of Christian revelation and the absolute correctness of theological interpretation. Both positions insist that true Christian faith involves the absence of all possible doubt regarding God's existence, nature, and revelation of Himself to man. It must be admitted that these positions have been, and still are, very widely held by orthodox Christians, Catholic and Protestant alike.

There is, however, another conception of Christian faith for which there is good authority in the Bible and in the thought of eminent Christians since New Testament times. It is suggested in Paul's statement, " Now we see through a glass, darkly . . . now we know in part," and it is stated explicitly by Pascal when he says, " If we must not act save on a certainty, we ought not to act on religion, for it is not certain. But how many things do we act on uncertainly . . . ! I say then we must do nothing at all, for nothing is certain, and that there is more certainty in religion than there is as to whether we may see tomorrow."[1]

This view of Christian faith assumes that it has all the essential characteristics of faith in general. Faith

[1] *Op. cit.*, Fragment 234.

may be defined as wholehearted belief on the basis of evidence, but not wholly conclusive evidence, and of interpretation which is reasonable, but which falls short of absolute proof. On this view, faith is never wholly blind, since it can be evoked only by what is at least to some extent experienced and apprehended. Nor is it ever completely enlightened, since that is the prerogative of omniscience, not of finite man. It is always somewhere between these two extremes— more or less informed, more or less blind and credulous. So defined, faith is essential to all human existence. For life necessitates continual decision and action, a continual taking of sides, in the absence of complete evidence and absolute proof. In so far as man is a rational being he would of course prefer never to decide and act save in the light of perfect knowledge, since, in an orderly world, every action and decision has its inevitable and inescapable consequences. But this is not given to finite man ; he must decide and act on faith, in every secular sphere as well as in religion. The scientist cannot prove with absolute certainty that the observed regularities of nature will prevail in the future ; he has to accept natural order on faith in order to investigate it. The humanist cannot be absolutely sure that man can improve his lot on earth ; only a faith in the possibility of such improvement can inspire him to continued humanistic effort.[1] Faith, secular or religious, involves " psychological " certainty when it is accompanied by no conscious doubts. It amounts to " moral " certainty when it is sufficient " for all practical purposes " and

[1] Thus, John Dewey quite properly raises the question as to " whether there are adequate grounds for faith [sic !] in the potentialities of human nature and whether they can be accompanied by the intensity and ardour once awakened by religious ideas upon a theological basis." He continues, " Is human nature intrinsically such a poor thing that the idea is *absurd ?* I do not attempt to give any answer, but the word *faith* is intentionally used. For in the long run democracy will stand or fall with the possibility of maintaining the faith and justifying it by works." *Freedom and Culture*, Allen & Unwin.

if it is resolute and unswerving. But it is never "logically" absolutely certain because faith and knowledge are not identical or coterminous and because man's knowledge is so incorrigibly finite that complete understanding is forever beyond his grasp.

Christian faith differs, on the view here defended, from secular faith primarily in the nature of the "object" to which it is directed and the resultant trust in and love for this "object." The "object" of Christian faith is not nature, or man, but God. God is not one among other objects if by "object" is meant a created "thing" or any part or all of our created universe. But God is the "object" of religious and Christian faith in the sense that such faith is a faith in God. Christian faith, in so far as it is enlightened, is based on evidence and interpretation of this evidence. But the evidence is distinctive and the proper interpretation of it is appropriate to its distinctive character. The relevant experiences are correctly described as "encounters" with the Deity in direct communion with Him and through His revelation of Himself to man in Jesus Christ. The relevant interpretation of these encounters is theological interpretation. In theology, reason goes as far as it can to give the most reasonable interpretation of God's nature and His relation to man. God's self-revelation is believed by Christians to be absolute in the sense of being wholly adequate to human needs. But men can understand this revelation only as finite beings, therefore only inadequately, never absolutely —sufficiently, Christians believe, to evoke their faith in God, to elicit their proper response to Him, and to lead them to express their proper attitude of love for their fellowmen with assurance—but, none the less, only with such assurance as is within the grasp of finite mortals. To deny this is to commit the fallacy of misplaced absoluteness.

There is, indeed, a philosophical sense in which God's reality can be said to be indubitable, namely, if He is defined from the outset as the ground of all being, the source and basis of all reality. No one, save an extreme solipsist, can deny the reality of God conceived of as the underlying condition of all existence and the " That " to which all human inquiry is ultimately directed. It is also appropriate to call this ultimate being " God " because Christianity, at least, conceives of God as absolute reality as well as in other ways. The factor of uncertainty enters in only when the further attempt is made to apprehend God's nature more specifically and to determine more concretely His relation to the universe and to man. This uncertainty, however, is of great importance for Christian faith, since the God of religious worship is never merely the " ground of all beings " but a Person worthy of our reverence, a God who so loves men as to evoke their responsible love. Christian faith in such a God is assured enough to enable Christians to live by it with complete confidence, but it must always fall short of absolute logical certitude.

Similarly, Christian faith, like all concrete religious decisions, is in one sense utterly convincing, but in another sense subject to the hazards and insecurities of any venturing faith. It involves, on the one hand, not only an utter commitment but a commitment that seems to the sincere Christian to be inescapable. For his experience of God is a compulsive experience ; he describes it as coercive, as a confrontation, as an experience so overwhelming, luminous, and meaningful that doubt regarding its spiritual validity and significance is unthinkable, an experience with such inner authority that no additional evidence could strengthen the faith which it generates. The assurance which characterizes this faith is of such a character as to make inappropriate such quantitative qualifications as

" more " and " less." Yet the fact remains that the criterion of " coerciveness " is, philosophically considered, not a sufficient criterion of reality or objectivity ; and the minute the other criterion of " coherence " is applied in the attempt to interpret the coercive religious experience meaningfully, the uncertainties inherent in all finite apprehension and decision are unavoidable. This is why Christian faith, however assured, *must* be a *venture* and why it must always fall short of absolutely certain knowledge, strictly defined.

The Bible and the Church are, for informed Christians, authoritative because they are man's chief objective sources for an understanding of God. The real authority of both is the spiritual authority of luminous and compelling insight. But man's interpretation of the Bible, as the chief record of God's Self-revelation, and the Church's interpretation of Christian doctrine remain finite and inadequate, however much these interpretations are inspired, or guided, by the Holy Spirit.

Dogmatism, as opposed to dogma, can then be defined as the denial of human finitude, the loss of proper humility, and the improper, indeed blasphemous, ascription to one's own beliefs, or to those of one's Church, of a degree of certainty which can actually characterize only the omniscience of God Himself. It is a manifestation of pride, both intellectual and spiritual, for it involves the deification of man and the absolutizing of his finite and relative knowledge. A Christian can believe that God is absolute without regarding his own conception of God as absolute or final. He can accept the authority of the Bible as the record of God's Self-revelation to man without regarding as finally authoritative his interpretation, or his Church's interpretation, of it. This sense of humility is desperately needed today, as always, in the Christian Church.

On the other hand, dogmas may, but need not, differ from religious dogmatism, for a dogma is a

H

belief basic to a given community, secular or religious. People cannot band together, share their experiences and work for a common end save on the basis of certain major presuppositions. In this sense, every community, including the Christian community, has its basic dogmas which constitute its credal frame of reference. Science has its dogmas or its creed—its basic faith, for example, in the uniformity of nature, and its unquestioned loyalty to scientific truth. Democracy presupposes the intrinsic value of man as man and the importance of justice and fair play. Similarly, Christianity, in each of the major and minor branches of the Christian Church, has its distinguishing dogmas. Inability to subscribe to the dogmas of any community, secular or religious, necessarily disqualifies one from membership in that community. This does not mean, however, that such dogmas cannot and should not be re-examined and revised from time to time by the community itself, since only thus is progress possible. This applies to the Christian Church. The steady development of Christian theology through the centuries shows that such re-examination and revision have actually taken place.

This interpretation of Christian dogmas, which Professor Thomas in Chapter III calls the " central affirmations " of Christianity, is not rationalistic but it is eminently reasonable. It does justice to man's finitude and sense of mystery, to God's Infinity, and to the Christian's faith in the adequacy of God's Self-disclosure. It also does justice to the principle of rationality in man and in the universe. Christian faith, it must be insisted, is not irrational, either in the sense of requiring man to suppress his reason or in the sense that God Himself is an irrational force. On the contrary, such rationality or order as exists in the universe is believed by Christians to be the creation of God and to reflect His character, and human reason

s conceived of as having been created by God for use.
What Professor Tillich has called " autonomous reason "
s reason fully aware of the ultimate rationality of man
and the world.   What may be called " theonomous
reason " is this same reason conceived of and operative
n the Christian perspective of God as the Source and
Ground of all reality.   Christianity is profoundly
committed to reason, *provided* it be used aright.   What,
hen, constitutes its abuse ?

4. *Original Sin*

No Christian dogma is more obnoxious to the secular
mind, whether naturalistic or humanistic, than that
of original sin.   It is particularly repellent when stated
n a mechanistic or legalistic form, as, for example,
hat we have all inherited at birth the sin incurred by
Adam.   But it is hardly more acceptable when stated
n more reasonable terms, namely, that there is in men,
n all men by virtue of their human and finite nature,
a fundamental egoism which impels them to value the
ower rather than the higher satisfactions of life, them-
elves rather than their fellowmen, mankind rather
han God.   On this view, sin is essentially idolatry, the
scription of supreme value to man and his works
ather than to God.   It is, in essence, alienation from
God.   " Sin is primarily the wrong attitude taken
oward God Himself. . . . It is the practical denial
of the fact that apart from personal communion with
God, human life is meaningless.   By sin the things a
person does, and the objectives he strives for, are
egarded as being of equal rank with communion
with God, and practically they take precedence over
hem."[1]   This sin is " original " because it is a deep-
eated tendency in all men, and the ultimate cause of
heir misery.   It is so fundamental that it cannot be

[1] Otto A. Piper, " The Biblical Understanding of Man," in *Theology Today*,
, 2, p. 194.

extirpated by a mere effort of will or by any merely human agency. It is also so fundamental that it perverts all human motives, directs reason to the wrong objectives, and thus progressively leads man further and further away from God. In terms of Professor Tillich's analysis, this misuse of reason is most evident in the irrationalism of Nazi totalitarianism, but it is also evident in the dedication of reason to technological advances as ends in themselves, and in the purely humanistic endeavour to make man as self-sufficient and autonomous as possible. For such striving for complete autonomy is, from the religious and Christian point of view, idolatrous. Reason is, in itself, good and not evil, but its use is good only if it is wisely used, and it is used wisely only within the ultimate religious and Christian perspective in which God is acknowledged to be supreme and communion with God is regarded as man's highest duty and felicity.

Is this an unreasonable analysis of human nature and destiny? It is, of course, if there be no God to whom man can dedicate his supreme devotion. But if the Christian apprehension of God is true it is hard to see how this Christian conclusion can be avoided. There is also much in secular experience, particularly today, that offers secular confirmation of this account of human sin. Is it not true that men, even in the best of health and in the happiest social environment, experience the loneliness of not being fully understood by any human being—a loneliness which an omniscient and loving Person alone could satisfy? Is it not true that there is something diabolical in men which makes them hurt what they most love, which gives them satisfaction in the misfortunes of others, however much they may despise themselves for this satisfaction whenever they become aware of it? Is it not true that, in the face of human hatred, violence, misery and injustice, the best of men, who in one sense are blameless for all

the institutional expression of this Christian community.

(b) A second objection points to the multiplicity of Christian Churches and the dogmatic insistence of some that they alone provide the true institutional expression of Christianity. The dogmatism of Christian Churches and their inclination to brand other Churches as more or less heretical must be admitted and bitterly deplored. Many Church people talk as though, if Jesus were to return to earth today, He would select the Church to which they belong as the only truly Christian Church. This attitude bespeaks an appalling lack of genuine Christian humility, a lack which sincere Christians should combat with all their strength.

On the other hand, a liberal humanist should be the first to honour the sanctity of man's conscience, particularly in matters of ultimate belief. He should also recognize the possibility of subscribing to a set of beliefs so whole-heartedly that he is willing to live for them and if necessary die for them, while acknowledging, in true humility, the inevitable inadequacy of his own beliefs and those of his Church, and the great likelihood that other Churches have achieved and preserved important Christian insights. A Christian can be loyal to his own Church without renouncing loyalty to the universal Church or looking with contempt or hatred upon those who, with equal sincerity, feel compelled to interpret and worship God in their own way. He can go further. In complete loyalty to the Christian Church, and to his own Church, he can and should also prize the spirit of religious humility and dedication in many who do not associate themselves with any Church and who may even oppose the Christian Church as such. He cannot agree with them, and he must remain convinced of their individual loss and their failure to make their humanistic endeavours more effective than they now are. But he can and should maintain toward them that respect to which all men are entitled as men and as the children of God.

(c) A third objection to the Church is occasioned partly by its use of language, partly by its ritualistic forms and practices. Again it must be admitted that Christians are, like other men, deplorably prone to employ words and phrases that have been worn threadbare, not by over-use but by abuse. The language they use is all too often a conventional jargon, a thoughtless parroting of phrases that have lost, for them and for their hearers, all significant meaning. It must also be admitted that any ritual tends to lose its significance through sheer repetition, and that its symbolic meanings, which once endowed it with expressive value, tend to be forgotten. In proportion as this happens, ritual becomes a type of mechanistic behaviour destructive of spirituality, or, even worse, behaviour regarded as productive of magical effects. These thoroughly unChristian abuses of language and rite in our Churches call today as always for recognition and reform.

Yet this secular objection may be the result of a lack of understanding of Christian thought and worship. It may, for example, reflect a failure to realize that all distinctive insights and truths can be expressed precisely only in an appropriate and adequate language, and that such a language must often include technical terms or common terms used in a distinctive way. No one today dreams of denying scientists the right to use a highly technical language. Why should a similar right be denied theologians? It may also be occasioned by a failure to appreciate the nature and function of religious ritual and by ignorance of the symbolic and expressive meaning of Christian rites.

But this only partly states and answers the difficulty. The real difficulty is that the secular mind has drifted so far from the Church, and the Church from contemporary interests and needs, that theological language and religious rites which were intelligible and meaningful to earlier generations have become, even when intelligently used, nearly meaningless to most people, including many Christians who attend church services fairly regularly. Even within the Christian Church there is a widespread failure today to recognize the fact that religious belief and dedication are expressed in many different languages, in the language of poetry and the arts as well as in the conceptual language of theology.[1] Hence the stupid insistence of narrow fundamentalists that the Bible be read as though its many poetic and prophetic passages were mere prose, to be taken as literalistically as possible. Hence also the common Protestant prejudice against ritual, as though it were necessarily inexpressive and magical.

The solution of this difficulty is not easy to find. Christian theologians must try to find fresh ways, meaningful to the modern world, to express old Christian truths and the relevance of these truths to the contemporary scene. They must also try to salvage and revivify well-established theological terms and symbolic rites which cannot be abandoned without serious loss. One of the great tasks of Christian education, within the Church and in Church-affiliated schools and colleges, is to promote a better understanding of the ways in which Christianity has been and can be expressed—in theology, in poetry, and in the visual and auditory arts.[2]

(d) A final objection to the Church is the unChristian character and behaviour of professing Christians. They are, so goes the criticism, hardly distinguishable from non-Christians in their attitudes toward their fellowmen and their preoccupation with secular pursuits and

[1] Cf. Richard Kroner, *The Religious Function of the Imagination*, Yale University Press, 1941.
[2] Cf. T. M. Greene, " Art as the Vehicle for Religious Worship," in *Religion in Life*, VII, 1, pp. 93 ff.

pleasures. Even the clergy are, with rare exceptions, condemned by the critical secularist as apparently lacking, to a deplorable degree, in that spirituality or essential piety which they, above all others, should manifest. The salt *has* lost its savour ; Christian faith seems no longer to produce that saintliness which informed sensitive humanists recognize and respect when they encounter it. In short, the worst enemies of the Christian Church are its own feeble and unfaithful members who so inadequately exemplify the Christian Gospel in their own lives.

It is this type of criticism, taken in conjunction with the admitted failure of the Christian Church to reach or touch the vast majority of folk even in Christian lands, which makes men like Laski and Mumford despair of the present or future effectiveness of the Christian Church. Mumford, for example, fully recognizes that science alone will not save us, that naturalism is a threat to human values, and that we stand in urgent need of a great spiritual revival. But he obviously has little confidence that this revival will come through the agency of the Church :

With all the talk of reunion between the Churches and sects, which has occupied the leaders of Christianity during the last half century, there are few real signs of the deeper spiritual effort required for Christianity's renewal—its admission of the local and relative nature of its original mission and its willingness to merge, for the sake of the universal values all men should share, with the faiths of other races and peoples which Western man too long spurned. An unChristian pride, disguising itself as a unique revelation of a truth not granted to other peoples, still blocks that essential sacrifice.[1]

Similarly, Laski recognizes the great social benefits

[1] Lewis Mumford, *op. cit.*, p. 376.

of Christianity in the past and the great contemporary
need for a faith that will revitalize the human mind.
But he feels compelled to turn to Communism, not
to Christianity, for this vitalizing faith :

> The Christian faith, in its period of power, . . .
> offered to the common man the secret consolation of
> heaven. But now that the basis upon which that faith
> was built has crumbled before critical examination,
> neither the Churches nor any other religious organiza-
> tion can hope to effect the work of renovation.[1]

These pessimistic estimates of the Church are the
result, in part, of secular beliefs which Christians
cannot share—Mumford's apparent belief that religious
people throughout the world should ignore the credal
differences which now separate them and subscribe to
some kind of eclectic world religion, and Laski's out-
spoken humanistic convictions and deep-seated religious
scepticism. But their assessment of the vitality, or lack
of vitality, of the Christian Church is impressive.
What can be said in answer to these charges ?

Our first answer must be a contrite *mea culpa*. We
are indeed miserable Christians, clergy and laity alike.
We are indeed our Church's worst enemies. Our faith
should indeed express itself in Christian works which
even the secular mind could recognize and respect.

But our critics are not wholly fair. For some of
them seem to believe that membership in a Christian
community should automatically transform sinners into
saints, or, alternatively, that only those who are already
saintly should be eligible for such membership. What
they forget is that it is man's bitter sense of sin that
drives him to Christianity, and that, though Christ
has promised us forgiveness, he has not promised to
transform us so radically that we will never sin again.

[1] Harold J. Laski, *Faith, Reason and Civilization*, Gollancz.

The Church ministers to sinners, and its ministry should be far more effective than it actually is ; but it has never pretended to relieve men of their sinful finitude. It is easy for us Christians to demand far too little of ourselves and of each other. It is equally easy for non-Christians to demand too much of us, indeed, to demand the impossible.

Our answer to those who remain aloof from the Christian Church because of its tragic faults must therefore be : Join us in the effort to correct these faults, not by criticism from the outside, valuable as such criticism is, but from the inside, where it can be constructive and healing. Think how immeasurably stronger and healthier the Church would be today if men and women like you—sincere, intelligent, courageous—were active members of the Church, loyal to its ideals and critical of its malpractices, determined to champion in it all that is truly Christian and to condemn with prophetic fury all that is pharisaical and idolatrous, zealous at whatever cost to purify Christian worship, clarify Christian thought, vitalize and redirect Christian practice—comrades with us in the common task of Christianizing Christendom.

But we must also say to them : Join us in order to receive as well as to give, to learn as well as to instruct, to confess your sins and repent and experience within yourselves the healing power of the Christian Gospel. For the Church is not *merely* a human association of men banded together to promote human ends ; it is also and essentially the association of men who acknowledge a common need, submit to a common judgment, and worship together a common Lord. It is, for all its faults, the vehicle of a great tradition in which are incorporated many spiritual insights to which you are still blind, the channel through which flow spiritual forces which are not now available to you. There are in the Church today many professing

Christians as sincere, intelligent and courageous as you, who constitute a truly Christian community of believers and who derive from this communal life something of the joy and the peace of Christian faith, worship and endeavour. If you join us in the right spirit, critically but humbly, contritely but hopefully, you will yourselves progressively enter into that experience which is the condition and the reward of Christian faith. You will learn to understand more profoundly the human values which you already cherish and to promote far more effectively the human ends to which you are already dedicated, because you will have new sources of illumination and power which you now lack.

No one can say with assurance how much inner vitality still remains in the Christian Church or what it can do to help an anguished world in a period of supreme crisis. There is certainly more genuine piety and spiritual vitality in the Church today than many secularists realize. There is certainly far less than there should be or might be. What Christians must assert is that, if Christianity be true, as they believe it is with all their hearts, they at least have no choice but to remain loyal to it and to redouble their efforts to make it more truly a Christian community. They must acknowledge the enormous difficulty of the task which they have set themselves and which they beg their secular brethren to share with them.

> To apprehend
> The point of intersection of the timeless
> With time, is an occupation for the saint—
> No occupation either, but something given
> And taken, in a lifetime's death in love,
> Ardour and selflessness and self-surrender.[1]

They must admit the actuality of what St. John of

[1] T. S. Eliot, *Four Quartets*, p. 27.

the Cross described as the " dark night of the soul,"
confess the inadequacy of their best apprehension of
God and of God's revelation to man, and acknowledge
the feebleness and fitfulness of their own spiritual life.
Eliot expresses this aspect of spiritual aspiration and
frustration, hope and endeavour in poetic language
which the sensitive secularist should be able to understand.

> For most of us, there is only the unattended
> Moment, the moment in and out of time,
> The distraction fit, lost in a shaft of sunlight,
> The wild thyme unseen, or the winter lightning
> Or the waterfall, or music heard so deeply
> That it is not heard at all, but you are the music
> While the music lasts. These are only hints and
>   guesses,
> Hints followed by guesses ; and the rest
> Is prayer, observance, discipline, thought and action.
> The hint half guessed, the gift half understood, is
>   Incarnation.[1]

They have no choice but to subscribe to Christianity's
ruthless judgment upon our secular society which,
while paying lip service to Christianity, has ignored
or repudiated what the Christian Church symbolizes
in the service of Holy Communion—a judgment which
Eliot has condensed into five savage lines.

> The dripping blood our only drink,
> The bloody flesh our only food :
> In spite of which we like to think
> That we are sound, substantial flesh and blood—
> Again, in spite of that, we call this Friday good.[2]

But they can also testify, in company with the

---

[1] *ibid.*
[2] *ibid.*, p. 16. Cf. T. M. Greene, " Beyond the Waste Land " in *Theology
Today*, I, 4, pp. 505 ff for an account of the religious content of this great poem.

prophets and the saints and in the light of their own
experience, to that peace of God which passeth all
secular understanding, to that joy and thanksgiving
which fill men's hearts and refresh them when, weary
and heavy-laden, they turn to Christ for forgiveness,
comfort, and strength.　At such moments they too are
impelled to cry with the Psalmist :

Make a joyful noise unto the Lord, all ye lands.
Serve the Lord with gladness : come before his presence
　　with singing.
Know ye that the Lord he is God : it is he that hath
　　made us and not we ourselves ; we are his people,
　　and the sheep of his pasture.
Enter into his gates with thanksgiving, and into his
　　courts with praise : be thankful unto him, and bless
　　his name.
For the Lord is good ; his mercy is everlasting ; and
　　his truth endureth to all generations.　(Psalm 100).

They too can say what St. Paul was able to say in the
anguish of his spiritual conflict :

For I am persuaded, that neither death, nor life, nor
　　angels, nor principalities, nor powers, nor things
　　present, nor things to come, nor height, nor depth,
　　nor any other creature, shall be able to separate us
　　from the love of God, which is in Christ Jesus our
　　Lord.　(Romans 8 : 38–9).

III

CENTRAL
CHRISTIAN AFFIRMATIONS

George F. Thomas

PROFESSOR TILLICH has analyzed the growing *predicament* of modern man which has resulted from his confident assertion of his autonomy: economic confusion, political tyranny, international anarchy, the disintegration of personality and community, the degradation of art and philosophy, and the weakening of religion by its association with a secular civilization. Though we may be convinced that there is still vitality in our American democracy, education, and religious and moral life, we must accept his analysis as a substantially true picture of the tendency of Western civilization as a whole and, with some qualifications, of our own.

It will avail us nothing to comfort ourselves in our optimistic American way by drawing large drafts on our hope for the future to balance our accounts with the past and present. We need not be frightened unduly by prophecies of inevitable doom. But if we are to overcome the tendency to disintegration in which we are involved, we must recognize the weakness of our foundations and resolutely set about the task of reconstructing them.

If the primary cause of disintegration is modern man's confidence in his own reason and will apart from responsibility to God, as Professor Tillich asserts, may not the *remedy* lie in a recovery of the theocentric view of life which has been impatiently brushed aside by the proud builders of secular modern culture?

The primary source of that view was the Christian faith. While the Church's understanding of the Christian faith has been weakened at many points by its compromise with modern thought and practice, Christianity still has the capacity to redeem modern life. Do not its central affirmations about God and His revelation, man and his sin, salvation, the Kingdom of God, and the meaning of history provide an answer to modern man's restless search for a centre of personal meaning and for a basis of community? Moreover, can they not be restated in terms which maintain continuity with traditional Christianity and at the same time preserve the achievements of the rational and liberal spirit of the modern world?

The purpose of this chapter is to attempt an answer to these questions. As Professor Greene has shown, there are many who are conscious of moral and spiritual need but who find it difficult to accept the Christian faith. Sometimes the reason is that they have come to accept a naturalistic or humanistic philosophy which makes it difficult if not impossible for them to consider seriously the Christian alternative. But sometimes the reason is to be found in an ignorance or misunderstanding of the Christian faith itself for which Christians themselves are partly responsible. Professor Greene has already dealt with some of the most common misconceptions of the Christian position. He has pointed out, for example, that Christian belief in the existence of God is not arbitrary and subjective but meets the ordinary criteria of objective reality: coerciveness, coherence with experience as a whole, and public verifiability. He has also pointed out that the " dogmas " or central affirmations of the Christian faith can be held without " dogmatism," while the denial of the Christian revelation on the ground that knowledge can be attained by the scientific method alone is itself in the highest degree " dogmatic." He

I

has therefore prepared the way for a restatement of the central affirmations of the Christian faith and of their relevance to human need. To that task this chapter is devoted.

I. REVELATION AND REASON

THE first great affirmation of the Christian faith is that the ultimate ground of existence and value is not an unknowable mystery but a *living God* who *has spoken* and *continues to speak* to men. It affirms that man knows the nature and purpose of God because God has disclosed Himself. It does not affirm, as has sometimes been said, that God has revealed Himself by overbearing our mental faculties. The faculty of reason is not superseded but raised to a higher level of vision under the influence of the divine inspiration. Christianity is opposed to the modern humanist belief in the autonomy of reason in so far as that belief flatters the pretensions of men to discover the nature and purpose of God without the aid of revelation. But it insists that the deepest truths about God and His purpose are revealed to men in and through all their faculties of reason, imagination, conscience, and feeling.

Why is reason without the aid of revelation unable to answer our ultimate questions about God and His purpose? The answer is, first, that the search for God by reason alone ends in the *identification of God with His works* or in *uncertain speculations about Him*, and, second, that God is of such a nature that He does not wait for man to find Him but *takes the initiative and discloses Himself* to man. It is worth while to explain briefly each of these points, since they prepare the way for the claim of Christians that God has actually sought out man and revealed Himself to him in history.

First, the statement that reason cannot attain to an

adequate knowledge of God by itself is not based upon general scepticism concerning the powers of reason. It rests upon the fact that reason apprehends the realities and values of the natural order more clearly than those of the supersensible order.

Now, God does not belong to the natural order to which reason is best adapted, either as a part of it or as the whole of it. If the testimony of the religious experience of mystic and plain man alike is to be trusted, He belongs to a higher, spiritual order of being and value which impinges upon the spatio-temporal order but is not exhausted by it. The claims of modern naturalistic thinkers like John Dewey that religious experience, referred in the past to a super-sensible Being, can without radical loss be directed toward a natural object such as man and his moral and social betterment are erroneous. In all high religious experience a vertical dimension of reality is disclosed and true worship is possible only when its Object is regarded by the worshipper as possessing an absolute worth unlike the relative value of any natural object. But since reason cannot grasp in " clear and distinct " ideas any object which transcends the natural order, men tend to substitute one or more of God's works in the natural order for Him. This is idolatry, whether it takes the form of ancient polytheism or modern deification of Nature, Beauty, State, Race, Utopia, or the ideal.

It is true that religious philosophers like Plato have sometimes risen above this tendency to idolatry by identifying the divine with an eternal and spiritual order above nature. But, noble as their speculations have often been, their inadequacy is illustrated by St. Augustine's remark in Book 7 of the *Confessions* that, while " the Platonists " believed in the Word, they did not know that the Word had become flesh, i.e., they had no conception of the redemptive work of God for sinful men. And philosophers like Aristotle who have been lacking in deep religious feeling have usually been led in their speculations to a metaphysical First Cause rather than to the God of religion.

But, second, while reason alone is unable to attain a convincing and adequate knowledge of God, by His very nature *God reveals Himself to men.* For God is *good*, and good by its very nature communicates itself. As Plato says in the *Timaeus*, the cosmos is a product of the goodness of the Creator which imparts itself to that which is other than itself. Especially if God is *living* and *personal*, as Christian experience indicates, He can be expected to disclose Himself to the finite persons who are His sons and who are in need of light for their darkness, as a human person in friendship willingly discloses himself to another person.

When general considerations such as these are taken into account the claim of Christians that as a matter of historical fact God *has* revealed Himself to man appears reasonable. The " special " historical revelation recorded in the Bible, it is true, does not stand alone but is the culmination of a " general " revelation in nature and history. Archbishop Temple has stated the point with great vigour : " Either all occurrences are in some degree revelation of God, or else there is no such revelation at all ; for the conditions of the possibility of any revelation require that there should be nothing which is not revelation."[1] If God is personal, Temple argues, His mode of operation must be *general* in order to maintain the stable order of events necessary for life and moral growth. On the other hand, revelation must also be *special* if it is to adapt itself to the needs of particular and changing historical situations and needs. For the action of a person responds to changing events and conditions in the process of realizing his purposes. To the deistic objection that

[1] *Nature, Man and God,* Macmillan, 1940, p. 306.

" general " revelation in the whole course of nature
and history is sufficient without appeal to " special "
revelation, we must reply that " general " revelation
says many and diverse things, as the long and often
strange procession of religions and philosophies witnesses.
A " special " revelation is therefore necessary both to
focus its meaning and give unity to it, and to raise it
to a higher level of purity ; and this revelation must
culminate *in* a person if it is to be an adequate revelation
to persons.

It cannot be denied that there is a deep *modern
prejudice* against this conception of a special historical
revelation through a particular series of events to
particular persons. There are a number of reasons for
this. One of the most important is the demand of
science for verification of every hypothesis by an appeal
to evidence accessible to every observer, since verification of this sort would appear to be possible only if the
data appealed to as evidence are general rather than
special. As Professor Greene has said, the Christian
experience which is the evidence for Christian revelation
is widespread and as such constitutes a public verification
of Christian beliefs, but it is restricted to those who are
able to receive it because they have met its moral and
spiritual conditions. Another reason is to be found in
the attempt of philosophy to grasp the ultimate nature
of reality in universal concepts rather than concrete
events and images. Closely related is the preference of
rationalists for timeless truths like those of mathematics
and logic which can be conceived in clear and distinct
ideas. All of this means that the dominant intellectual
tradition of Western thought has stressed knowledge of
the *universal* aspects of experience and of the *unchanging*
structures of reality rather than knowledge of *unique and
changing temporal events*. But the influence of historical
method and of evolutionary theory has been for over
a century modifying this in favour of more dynamic

conceptions. If *time* is taken seriously and nature is conceived in terms of *process*, we may find in particular historical events and persons our best insight into the universal meaning and purpose of things. For movement in time toward ends is best understood by insight into the meaning of the most illuminating special phases of the movement of history. The modern prejudice against an historical revelation, therefore, is a product of scientific and philosophical rationalism and cannot stand in the face of the empirical facts of history.

On the other hand, it is a serious mistake to suppose that belief in a special divine revelation in history is incompatible with appreciation of the *value of human reason*. Not only must Christians accept the autonomy of reason in dealing with the facts and laws of the natural order ; they must also employ reason in the working out of the theoretical and practical implications of their faith. They must, therefore, come to terms with and make full use of the conclusions of scientists and philosophers. One or two examples will make this clear. The Christian belief that the natural order owes its existence, its regularity, and its value to God is fully compatible with the most careful scientific investigation of the laws of nature. Indeed, at its best it has itself strengthened interest in natural science by enhancing the value of nature as the handiwork of God and a striking manifestation of His wisdom. Again, the revelation through Christ that man's duties to his fellows depend upon love of God and his neighbour demands the most patient effort to understand our neighbours individually and collectively, and to make full use of psychology and the social sciences for that purpose. For revelation does not settle automatically all questions which arise concerning nature and human life. As it has come to men in the past in specific historical situations, so it requires to be applied to the specific situations of our own time with

the help of all the knowledge that is available. It
gives full scope, therefore, to the interest of scientists
in the structure of nature and to the efforts of the
descriptive and normative sciences of man, such as
psychology and political science, which are so essential
to human welfare.

II. THE BIBLICAL REVELATION

WHAT, now, is the Christian idea of the special
historical revelation of God recorded in the *Bible*?
It has been so often misconceived that it is necessary
to speak briefly of its purpose, method, content, and
use.

As to its *purpose* God has revealed Himself, not
primarily to *enlighten the minds of men*, but to *bring them
into fellowship with His own life* and *obedience to His will*.
Only so can their lives be transformed, only so can
their dignity as sons of God made in His image be
attained, only so can they be brought to take their
place in His creative and redemptive purpose. Religion
is both theory and practice, but it is primarily practice.
It does not provide answers to all our problems, it
bestows life upon us. In short, revelation is for the
sake of liberation, redemption, salvation. That is why
to Christians the person and redemptive work of Jesus
of Nazareth constitute the supreme act of revelation
and the culmination of the whole process of general
and special revelation. Only through the life of a
person, as we have said, could God speak fully and
clearly to human persons. The earlier revelation in
the lawgivers, prophets, and wise men of the Old
Testament cannot be dispensed with. But the significance of that revelation is thrown into higher relief
and its partial insights are brought to fulfilment in
Christ. Moreover, since it is the love and redemptive
purpose of God which are revealed in Christ, we must

look to his *whole* personality, words and deeds, life and death, spirit and influence alike, for that revelation.

Its *method* is not, as fundamentalists claim, the communication of divine truths to passive minds whose natural faculties are superseded by the Divine Spirit and whose very words are dictated to them. This naïve view of inspiration is unworthy of a God who deals with His sons not as puppets but as persons, and it depreciates the genius of the prophets to whom God speaks. Rather, revelation comes to men who are actively seeking light in their darkness to guide their people and who bring to bear all of their faculties of feeling, imagination, and reason. It is *mediated by historical events* as interpreted by such men. This does not mean, of course, that inspiration cannot come in quiet meditation and relative detachment from external happenings, much less that the meaning of historical events is written upon them so clearly that the personal interpretation of the prophet is unessential. But it does mean that God speaks to the human spirit in deeds as well as words. The prophet sees Him at work in the migrations of peoples, the fall of empires, the rise of great leaders, in short, the destruction of the evil and the exaltation of the good in history. Thus, the method of revelation involves both an *objective* factor of divine judgment upon evil and redemption of good in history and a *subjective* factor of interpretation by the inspired prophet.

What is the *content* of revelation? It is not, as dogmatists have said, articles of faith, propositions which state truths about God and His Will in final and unalterable words. What is revealed is both more and less than dogmas or propositions. It is more because God reveals *Himself*, not mere *ideas* about Himself. The prophet experiences the living presence and action of God in fellowship with Him. It is also less because the nature and purpose of God so

experienced is only *partially grasped* by the prophet.
Though the revelation is real, the veil of mystery is
never wholly torn away. Among other things, this
means that faith, the response of man's whole being
to God as revealed, is required if the revelation is to
be accepted ; and it is always possible to deny it on
the ground that its reality or meaning is not transparent
to reason. It also means that the revelation to a
particular prophet is never so comprehensive, the
interpretation put upon it by himself and others never
so adequate, that later revelation and interpretation
are unnecessary.

If this conception of the purpose, method, and
content of the biblical revelation is accepted, it
involves several important corollaries as to the *use* of
the Bible. (1) The first is that the Bible is not itself
the revelation but the record of the revelation. This
sets us free from Bibliolatry. It enables us to look
beyond the words to the meaning, to appeal from
the *letter* to the *spirit*. (2) The second is that the
fundamentalist dogma of the infallibility or inerrancy
of every word and book of the Bible is false. For its
revelation, we said, has come through historical events
as interpreted by inspired men whose personal faculties
were active in the process. This means that the
Divine Word which was originally spoken cannot be
simply identified with the human word which was
written by the inspired prophet. Therefore, *discrimination* must be exercised in interpreting and applying
to our own lives the revelation recorded in the Bible.
It is not equally true and equally binding in all its
parts. (3) The third corollary is that the biblical
revelation is not final in the sense of exclusive. If
God is the Father of all humanity, as He is revealed
in the Bible, He could not have left Himself without
a witness among any of the peoples of the earth or
failed to guide the Church through the ages into *new*

truth by the Spirit. Part of the reaction against the Bible in the modern period has been due to the narrowness of those who have insisted that God could be found only in the Scriptures.

This view of revelation enables the modern Christian to hold a spiritual conception of the *authority* of the Bible. Its authority lies not in the holiness of the book itself not in its verbal inerrancy or monopoly of truth, but in the *inherent validity* of its record of divine initiative and disclosure as a whole over a period of more than a thousand years. Its authority is spiritual in the sense that it awakens and satisfies the deepest spiritual needs of men, winning their assent without the necessity of appealing to external proofs. But since some of its passages and books are not up to the high level of inspiration of the Bible as a whole, the Christian must use it with critical judgment and freedom as a source of light and power, rather than as a set of theological dogmas or a manual of moral rules to be followed slavishly.

But the modern, critical view of the biblical revelation must never lead us to overlook its *paradoxical* character. To say that the divine revelation commends itself by its own spiritual power as reasonable is not to say that the divine " wisdom " has ever been anything other than " foolishness " to the reason of the " natural " man. The great revelation of the anonymous prophet of the exile[1] that Israel's sufferings were laid upon her for the healing of the sinful nations which had oppressed her was not accepted by all or even by most of his fellow-exiles. Its sublime humility and faith had their effect upon those who were able to transcend national particularism and gain a universal outlook ; and it enabled the early Church to understand the suffering of Christ and to accept its missionary task to the Gentile world. But to most Jews and Christians to this day the idea of national suffering undergone for

[1] Isaiah, chs. 40 ff.

the healing of the nations still seems alien and irrational. Similarly, Jesus' teaching that the " poor in spirit " and the " meek " are truly " blessed," that God loves the sinner as well as the righteous, and that to " save " life one must " lose " it involves such a radical transvaluation of ordinary values that it strikes the " natural " or " fleshly " man (to use St. Paul's term) as contrary to common sense.   Above all, the central affirmations of the Bible that God not only forgives repentant sinners but longs for their return to Him and actively enters into the arena of human life in order to redeem them has always been a " scandal " to Jews and " nonsense " to Gentiles.

Because of this paradoxical character of the Christian revelation, the proper attitude toward it is one of *faith*, the active response of the whole man to supersensible Reality and Good as revealed in religious experience. There can be no legitimate objection to such faith from the point of view of reason.   The function of reason is not to legislate for reality, divine or otherwise, but to accept every disclosure of reality from whatever source it comes.   It cannot create knowledge by itself ; as it depends upon materials derived from sensation for its knowledge of the natural world, it must depend upon religious experience and insight for its knowledge of supersensible Reality and Good.   If it judges the divine nature and purpose by ideas derived solely from experience of the natural world, it is bound to fall into error.   For example, to the legalists of Jesus' time it seemed that God's justice must be like man's, that He must pay the workers in His vineyard according to the length of their work ;   but Jesus reveals (Mt. 20 : 1-15) that the rewards of the Kingdom are bestowed by God without reference to such human standards. Much of the " irrational " and " paradoxical " character of revelation is due simply to men's judging it by the standards of unredeemed " natural " men who have had no religious experience and insight that could prepare them to understand it.

As we shall see later, the reason of the "natural" man is also prevented from attaining such insight by the distortion of its vision through sin. But there is no inherent necessity for it to reject the one source by which light can come to it from the spiritual order. Indeed, the reason of the "spiritual" man has always responded to the great sayings and deeds of the Bible. It transcends the limited views and interests of the "natural" man's reason and approves the higher truth and goodness revealed to it. Thus, he who "has the Spirit" can "discern spiritual things."

Therefore, it is wrong to insist too much upon the primacy of the *volitional* element in faith, "the will to believe." Since faith goes beyond the evidence of sense, and since it involves trust and commitment as well as assent, the volitional element is important. But men do not lay hold of faith ; faith lays hold of them. It is not an achievement of their will, but comes to them as a "gift of God." Since it is a *response of the whole personality to the revelation of God*, faith is far from being an arbitrary act of will. But the volitional aspect is necessary, since one must be willing to commit oneself and maintain his faith in the face of much in life that may suggest doubt and even on occasion drive him to the brink of despair. For faith must struggle with the difficulties that confront the divine action in history. It lays hold upon the ideal as the eternally real ; but it is painfully aware of the gulf between the ideal and the actualities of history within which man must live.

III. GOD

So much for the nature and necessity of revelation, its relation to reason, the special revelation recorded in

the Bible, and the faith that lays hold upon that
revelation. What is disclosed in the biblical revelation
about *God*? The crucial importance of that question
is best realized when we bear in mind the doubts and
difficulties of contemporary naturalists and humanists,
as Professor Greene has described them. Modern man
cries out in his doubt, " Is the ultimate reality anything
but a blind, purposeless energy whose movements are
governed by necessity and are utterly indifferent to
human weal and woe ? What right do we have to
believe that behind the processes of nature and history
there is a God whom we can trust and who will help
us in our need ? " The biblical answer to this question
is not a speculative proof of the existence and goodness
of God ; it is a revelation of God in history reaching
its climax in Christ's manifestation of His redemptive
love. What does the Bible affirm about God?

The primary biblical affirmation about God is that
He is at once eternal Creator of nature and sovereign
Will working out His righteous purposes in history.
All things depend upon Him as their Creator and
Sustainer ; all men depend upon Him as their
Redeemer. He is thus *Lord of all creation* and *Father
of all men*. The modern denial of nature's dependence
upon God and man's responsibility to Him is the root
of the humanistic dogma of the self-sufficiency of man.
It is the source of the rationalistic belief in the adequacy
of human reason, unaided by divine revelation, to
discover ultimate truth, and in the power of the human
will without divine grace to attain ultimate good. It
is necessary, therefore, to realize how profoundly this
primary affirmation about God has affected man's
conception of his own nature and destiny, if we are
to see clearly what its denial has meant to modern
man.

Clearly, the God who is revealed in the Bible is not
the God of speculative philosophers but the God of

religion. It is not God as He is *in His essence* apart
from the world; rather, it is God *in His relation* to
nature and man. The Bible shows little interest in
philosophical speculation about the nature of God in
His inmost essence; its interest is in the *action of God*
upon His creatures and especially upon man. Of
course, the revelation of God in and through His acts
leads to a partial knowledge of His essence, for His
acts are the expression of His essence. If He lays down
righteous laws for His people, it is because He is
righteous; if He shows mercy toward them, it is
because He is loving; if His glory is too bright for
mortal and sinful man to behold, it is because He is
holy. But it is significant that God is always represented
in action, not in a Sabbath rest of self-sufficient
perfection.

The reason for this reticence about God's inner
essence is doubtless to be found partly in a deep sense
of awe before the mystery, the majesty, the " otherness "
of the Holy One. It is also an expression of the
intensely practical character of Hebraic and Christian
religion, which stresses moral obedience to the divine
Will far more than mere contemplation of the divine
attributes. But it is ultimately due to a still deeper
cause : the vivid realization that God's perfection is
not static but dynamic, nor the mere *possession* of all
being and goodness in undisturbed calm, but the
communication of His being and goodness to that which
is other than Himself. For the God revealed in the
Bible is the very antithesis of the detached and self-
sufficient Prime Mover of Aristotle. Indeed, He has
little in common with the utterly transcendent God of
certain passages of the great *Summa* of St. Thomas
Aquinas, a God who creates the world but who is not
related to the world in such a way as to be affected
by it. Doubtless this Greek and Scholastic way of
thinking has its element of value, since the world is

not necessary to God in the same sense as God is necessary to the world. The world depends upon God as the conditioned upon the unconditioned, the derivative upon the ultimate ; and in this sense God does not depend upon the world. But according to the biblical revelation, it is the nature of God to create, to communicate His being and goodness to creatures, to go out of Himself in order to pour His life into that which is beyond Himself. Moreover, it is His nature to care for that which He has created, to sustain it continuously in being, and to redeem it from evil and destruction. In this sense, God apart from His relation to nature and man would not be God.

The implications of this view of God are far-reaching. It is what makes possible the conception of revelation we have already analyzed. For such a God is to be met, not primarily in the intellectual contemplation of those who have elevated themselves by the discipline of detachment above the struggles and changes of time, but on the dusty highways of history and in the crises of moral struggle. A God who is dynamic, outgoing, active, does not wait to be discovered ; He discloses Himself. Again, His activity is *creative*, ever bringing into being new opportunities for His sons. He discloses Himself especially in those crucial situations of personal and social life which lay bare its deepest issues, confronting men and nations with judgments and calling them to higher possibilities. He calls Abraham to leave his native land and go to a land of promise utterly unknown to him. He commands Moses to deliver his people from a bondage from which escape seemed impossible. He raises up " judges " or heroes to free Israel from her oppressors in Canaan. He speaks oracles of woe through Amos upon unjust Israel as well as upon her neighbours. He inspires Isaiah with a vision of a Messianic era of righteousness and peace. In short, He is the *Lord of History*, working through

men and nations whom He has raised up to fulfil His
purpose. As men and nations respond to His call in
faith and surrender their wills to His purpose, they
are raised by His spirit above themselves and enabled
to do marvellous deeds.

Second, we must notice the *character* and *direction* of
this creative activity. The biblical writers do not say
that God is concerned only with man, but they have
no doubt of man's special place in the Creation and
in the purposes of the Creator. The reason for this,
as far as it lies in the nature of man, we shall consider
in the next section. The essential thing here is that
God's will is a *holy will*, His purpose a *righteous purpose*.
This is sometimes misconceived by moralists who see
in religion little more than a means of assurance that
God will conserve and enhance the values prized by
men as they are. But the biblical writers emphasize
the fact that God, not man, is the measure of good
and evil. It is His will which defines what is righteous ;
men must submit themselves to His laws. His demands
are far more exacting than those of conventional
morality ; the justice and inexorableness of His judgments are emphasized again and again.

But He is also *merciful* and *forgiving*. He is full of
loving-kindness. He must punish Israel for her infidelity
to her covenant with Him and her injustice to the poor,
but He longs for her to repent and return to Him. He
knows the frailty of man and shows compassion upon
him in his sins. This conception of God's righteous
Will in terms at once of stern justice and tender mercy
ennobled the moral ideals of the Hebrews in a striking
way. Under the influence of the prophets, the moral
demands of God upon His people came to include
both a high standard of justice between men and a
broad humanitarianism which is especially considerate
of the widow, the fatherless, the stranger, and the poor.
In a fine passage in which Job defends his moral

integrity, justice and kindness take a central place :

> I was eyes to the blind,
> And feet was I to the lame.
> I was a father to the needy ;
> And the cause of him that I knew not I searched out.
> And I brake the jaws of the unrighteous,
> And plucked the prey out of his teeth.
>
> (Job 29 : 15–17)

> If I did despise the cause of my manservant
> Or of my maidservant, when they contended with me ;
> What then shall I do when God riseth up ?
> And when he visiteth, what shall I answer Him ?
> Did not he that made me in the womb make him ?
>
> (Job 31 : 13–15)

Passages like these show how far beyond a merely conventional and legal morality the greatest Hebrews had gone before the Christian era. The further step needed was Jesus' profound teaching that a perfect and redemptive love like God's is the source of all true goodness, the fulfilment of the law.

Third, we must notice briefly the *ultimate goal* of the creative, righteous, and merciful will of God. For hope for divine redemption in the future as well as belief in the divine initiative in the past distinguishes the biblical revelation. The transformation of the " Messianic hope " from its simple nationalistic and earthly beginnings into Jesus' Gospel of a universal and spiritual " Kingdom of God " will be dealt with in the last section of this chapter. The important thing to note here is that in these hopes for the future the righteous Will of God is revealed to be, not merely a transcendent standard by obedience to which individual men are to be judged in heaven, but a living activity bent upon the realization of a community of justice and peace through history. God is concerned with the issues of time and history. He is no mere

K

eternal and immutable Ideal of Goodness which men must seek to discover and imitate in their lives, but a Creative Will bent upon overcoming the obstacles that confront the ideal among the actualities of history. And He has the power to carry out His purposes despite these obstacles.

Fourth, the " metaphysical " attributes of God are also important, indeed, they are essential to the religious and moral point of view of the Bible. If God were not *transcendent*—" high and lifted up," as He appears in Isaiah's vision—He could not be regarded as superior to the finite and imperfect creatures of nature and history. If He were not *eternal,* there would be no stable and permanent factor in time, and history would be a meaningless flux. If He were not *immutable* in the direction of His purpose toward a definite end, without " variableness " or " shadow of turning," His will could not be depended upon and human hope would be in vain. These " metaphysical " attributes, however, must never be understood in Greek fashion as those of a static, self-sufficient, impassive Being. They are attributes of a creative living Spirit. If they are separated from the " moral " and " personal " attributes of justice and mercy and purpose, they transform the Christian God of history into the timeless and changeless Being of Greek philosophy.

On the other hand, the Christian is or should be fully aware that in attributing a " *moral* " and " *personal* " character to God, he is only using an analogy derived from imperfect human beings. Any suggestion of naïve anthropomorphism must be corrected and the limitations that belong to human personality must be removed from his conception of God. A long line of Christian philosophers and mystics have warned that the infinite and eternal God cannot be comprehended fully by any concept or symbolized adequately by any analogy. But despite all the difficulties and dangers involved in

" personalizing " their thought of the Divine, Christians have always found it necessary to do so in order to express the *living* and *responsive* character of God as they have experienced Him. Moreover, only in this way can their thinking about Him be prevented from lapsing into utter vagueness and agnosticism, on the one hand, or materialistic and sub-personal conceptions, on the other.

IV.　CREATION, MAN AND SIN

THE second affirmation of Christianity has to do with man, his relation to nature and to God, and his sin. The doctrine of man is dependent upon the doctrine of the *Creation*. Christianity is opposed to the naturalistic view of nature as all-inclusive and self-explanatory, the product of blind purposeless forces moving by necessity, and to the view of man as simply a child of nature, a species of the animal kingdom whose destiny is fulfilled wholly on earth. It affirms that nature as a unified and orderly whole owes its existence to the wisdom and power of God, and that man both belongs to nature and transcends nature.

According to the critical conception of revelation previously described, the story of the Creation in the first chapter of Genesis is to be taken, not as a scientific description, but as a sublime and inspired philosophical myth constructed by the Hebrew religious imagination at its best. It asserts the dependence of the visible cosmos and its order upon the creative intelligence and will of God. It also suggests the purpose of the Creation : the realization of good in various kinds of creatures, inanimate, animate, and human, each " according to its kind." Finally, it culminates in the making of man as " lord " of the Creation, exalted above other creatures by the fact that he alone has been made in the " image " of God. In the same spirit, the author of the eighth Psalm says about man, " Thou hast made him a little lower than the angels, and hast crowned him with glory and honour." At the same time, the existence and value of the Creation and man are derivative. Men are utterly dependent upon the eternal Creator for all they are and all they enjoy. This is symbolized vividly by the moulding of man (in the earlier myth found in Genesis, ch. 2) out of the dust of the earth, as if to emphasize the fact that he is as finite and mortal as all other creatures.

Thus, the myth of the Creation serves the double religious purpose of affirming the *value of the world and of man* and of reminding man of his *dependence upon and responsibility to his Maker*. Nature as a whole, matter and form, body and spirit, has been created by the eternal Source of all good for a good purpose. This means, on the negative side, that every ascetic idea of the evil of the body and its appetites is ruled out. It means, on the positive side, that human interest in the order of nature, enjoyment of her beauty, and grateful use of her resources are wholly justified. In more religious terms, it means that nature as a whole is a " sacramental " system, a worthy vehicle for the communication of the Divine Spirit with human spirits and for the fulfilment of the purposes of both.

But this is conditional upon man's *acknowledgment of God* as the Lord of nature and as the Father to whom he owes filial obedience. For that which is distinctive of man is, not only that he depends upon God for his " creation, preservation, and all the blessings of this life," but that he can gratefully acknowledge his dependence and his responsibility. This capacity is his because he is a spiritual being. As such, he is able to transcend nature, enter into communion with God, and freely subject himself to His will.

The foundation of the *spiritual* nature of man is his capacity to apprehend supersensible Reality and Good.

It is through this capacity that he lays hold of the revelation of God to him. The activity of the Spirit in him gives rise to faith, and from this faith springs love in the Christian sense of the term. The direction of his love, St. Augustine says, determines the character of a man ; like a weight it draws him irresistibly toward its object. Therefore, if love is directed by faith toward God as ultimate Truth and Good, the soul is raised above itself and attains its true fulfilment and peace ; but if it is directed toward the self, it misses its blessedness. In brief, man as a spiritual being is capable of hearing the call of God, responding to it by faith, and showing forth his faith in acts of love.

According to the classical and modern view of humanism, the most distinctive thing about man is that he is a *rational* being, able to discover truth by himself and to determine his conduct by ends he sets for himself. This is true as a description of that which distinguishes man from the lower animals. It is also important for Christians to assert man's rationality against every form of modern irrationalism such as that of Freud, though it is an error to identify reason with reasoning as is done by modern rationalistic thinkers. The Greek conception of reason as partici- pating in the rational structure of the cosmos and hence as capable of intuiting ultimate truth and value is needed both to check the excesses of modern rationalism and to overcome the irrationalism which has arisen in reaction against it.

But Christians cannot accept the view that man's rationality is all that is meant by the " image of God " in him, since this would exalt a natural function of man in and for itself. The natural functions of reason, will and affection are of worth only in so far as they are used in the service of the Divine Will and its creative and redemptive purpose. Therefore, the

" image of God " in man consists not only of his rational capacity to intuit ultimate truth and value but also of his capacity for faith and love.

Moreover, the Christian view recognizes the *complexity* of human nature more clearly than the classical humanistic view. It avoids both the " reductionistic " tendency of naturalism (by its stress upon the spiritual aspect of man) and the " perfectionistic " tendency of romantic idealism (by its realistic recognition of human finitude and sin). It asserts that man occupies a middle position on the scale of being. In comparison with the mighty forces of nature, he seems a weak and helpless creature whose life is at the mercy of the elements. But though he is only a " reed," as Pascal says, he is a " thinking reed " : by his consciousness he transcends all the powers of nature in dignity. Hence, both his " greatness " and his " misery " must be asserted and asserted together. He is neither angel nor brute, but seems to have something of both in himself. By contrast with this recognition of the *duality* in man, secular thinkers of the modern period have tried to deny both the high and the low in man by minimizing his soaring aspirations as " fantastic " and excusing his shameful misdeeds as " natural."

It is because of its deeper understanding of this complexity in the nature of man that Christianity takes more seriously than humanism does the *problem of sin.* It affirms that man's spiritual nature has been corrupted by egoism, pride and sensuality. As a result, his natural faculties have been perverted and are in need of transformation by the divine grace. His reason is no longer able to attain to the highest truth about God and His will ; his will is powerless to follow perfect Goodness ; his affections are set upon inferior and transitory pleasures. There is no evil inherent in these natural faculties ; they belong to the rational nature of man as part of a good Creation. St. Augustine, for example,

rejects[1] the Stoic view that the passions which disturb
our tranquillity are evil.   Pity and sorrow, as well as
love, have an important function to perform and are
good in so far as they are directed toward the right
objects.   But as the result of sinful egoism, all of them
have been in a measure perverted and deflected from
their true uses.   Thus, man contradicts his spiritual
nature by his sin.   Cut off from their true object and
purpose, his natural capacities become instruments of
what St. Paul calls the " flesh " rather than the " spirit,"
servants of self-love rather than love of God and love
of neighbour.   As a result of this contradiction and
perversion, man falls prey to inner discord, strife with
his fellows, and profound misery.

If this analysis of the inner contradiction in man is
accepted, the necessity of a *radical change* to reconcile
him to God and to restore him to his true self is
inescapable.   Modern man has attempted to deny this
necessity by asserting his dignity as a rational being
and by denying his bondage to sin.   As Professor Tillich's
essay has shown, however, his proud claim to autonomy
has only led to the destruction of personality and community throughout our Western world.   The fundamental reason for this destruction becomes clear when
we look at it from the perspective of the Christian view
of man.   Both individualism and collectivism in the
modern world are results of the separation of man by
sin from the Divine Ground of all meaning and value.
Responsible no longer to God, the individual has sometimes found meaning for his life in relatively disinterested
service to intrinsic values, such as scientific truth or
beauty ; and many have found satisfaction in promoting
the welfare of class, nation, or humanity.   But neither
realization of value nor concern for social welfare can
have its fullest meaning without relation to the eternal
purposes of God.   Moreover, in the absence of any

[1] *City of God*, Book XV.

generally accepted definition of the highest good, men and groups have followed their own desires and interests. The inevitable result has been widespread frustration and bitter strife.

To modern man suffering from this emptiness of his life apart from God, from his true self, and from his fellows, there is offered once more the Christian way of *reconciliation* to God through Christ. To the individual salvation can come only as he puts his ultimate trust, not in himself and his " values," nor in his group, but in God and His love. It is as true of modern Europeans and Americans as it was of the ancient Jews and Greeks that they cannot find peace and joy in the multiplicity of their " good works " or the greatness of their social " achievements." What they need above everything is a faith which will enable them to overcome their fear and anxiety, their pride and sensuality, their self-centredness and isolation.

The only faith which can do this is faith in the willingness of God to forgive them their sins and to give them by His grace the love that casts out fear and selfishness. What can awaken in them this faith in God's willingness to forgive and to grant them the power for a new life ? Here again the answer of Christianity is not to be found in any discovery by science or speculative philosophy. It is to be found in the *actual experience of forgiveness and new life through Christ*. This is the answer Christians have always given to the question, " How can man be reconciled to God and win a victory over sin and the spiritual death it brings ? " It is for this reason that the affirmations of Christians about Christ and his work of reconciliation are of crucial importance for an understanding of the Gospel.

V. CHRIST AND THE CREEDS

THE affirmation of Christians about Jesus of Nazareth, his nature, his redemptive work, and the new life bestowed upon men by union with his Spirit is the most distinctive thing in their faith. They have always believed that his life and death are fully understood only when they are viewed as manifestations of the *redemptive power of God incarnate in a perfect man*. This conviction found its earliest expression in the " confession " by Peter at Cæsarea Philippi, " Thou art the Christ," i.e., the " Messiah " or ideal King to be sent by God to free the righteous Israelites from their evil oppressors. Soon after Jesus' death his followers came to think of him, not merely as the Jewish " Messiah " sent to redeem Israel, but also as their heavenly " Lord " through faith in whom salvation must come to men. As they spread the " Gospel " or good news abroad and Gentiles began to accept it in large numbers, he came to be regarded more and more as the " Son of God " sent to redeem all men, the " Saviour " of Jew and Gentile, male and female, bond and free. What was the cause of this remarkable exaltation of the person of the Galilean ?

It was, of course, the vivid impression made by him during his earthly career which was the starting-point for these exalted views of him and his work. But it was also—and even more for men like St. Paul who had probably not known him " after the flesh "—the consciousness of the profound *change wrought in their lives* by faith in him and union with his Spirit. Liberation from sin and despair had been accompanied by love and joy and peace. In wonder and gratitude they could only give to Christ the glory. Thus, the experience of salvation through Christ, rather than abstract theological speculation for its own sake, is the primary source of the high views of his person in the early Church.

In Colossians he is pictured as existing before his earthly career as a heavenly being and it is said that in him " the entire fullness of deity has settled bodily " (Col. 2 : 9). According to the Fourth Gospel he was the incarnation of the eternal " Word " which was in the beginning with God, was the source of light and life in the world, and finally took flesh in order to bring eternal life to men.

These statements are all the more striking because they were made by men who would not have thought of denying the unity and sovereignty of God the Father. They saw in Christ the Son of the one God who derives his being and authority from the Father and subordinates himself to Him. In short, the exaltation of Christ by the early Christians was not meant as a speculative dogma about a second God but as a solemn and grateful affirmation that the one and only " God was in Christ reconciling the world to himself."

It is in the light of this experience that we are to understand the *Trinitarian conception* of God. Why have Christians always felt that, difficult as it is to conceive, the Trinitarian view of God has a profundity that is lacking in the abstract monotheism of Judaism and Mohammedanism ? The reason is that the activity of God as Creator and Ruler of the world appears different from His activity as Redeemer of mankind in Christ and that both appear different from His activity as the indwelling Spirit which inspires the lives of those who put their trust in Him. The doctrine of the Trinity is an assertion of the reality of these ways in which God shows Himself to Christians, and an insistence upon the source of them in the eternal being of God. Historically, it arose out of the conviction of Christians that in Christ the Divine had decisively entered into human life and that the process of redemption thus begun had been continued in the lives of his followers by the Holy Spirit of God. It meant that God was truly and fully revealed both in Christ and in the Spirit, that no mere *temporary modes* but *eternal aspects of the Divine Being* were manifested in them. Philosophically, the doctrine has also served to free Christians from the tendency of abstract monotheism to picture God as simple and undifferentiated unity utterly separated from the rich diversity of the world. It symbolizes the diversity within unity of God : His transcendent Sovereignty, redemptive Love, and indwelling spiritual Presence.

The danger of the Trinitarian formula, " one Substance in three Persons," has always been that the *eternal aspects* of the Divine activity tend to be taken as *independent centres* of consciousness and volition, as " persons " in the modern sense of individual entities with a substantial existence of their own. This tritheism has been far from the minds of the greatest thinkers of the Church, especially Athanasius, the father of Nicene theology, and Augustine, the greatest Latin exponent of it. But popular Christianity easily falls into tritheism when it centres devotion in turn upon the different " Persons " of the Godhead. For this reason it is necessary for Christians to emphasize the fact that God is *one* Personal Being.

If the original meaning of the terms used at Nicaea is understood, much of the difficulty disappears. The word we translate as " person " (" hypostasis " in Greek or " persona " in Latin) meant more than a temporary " mode " of the Godhead but less than a " person " in our sense of the term. There are not three subjects or centres of consciousness in God ; rather, there is one Personal Being who exists and manifests Himself in three eternal aspects or functions. Above all, we must remember that the primary purpose of the Nicene theology was religious rather than philosophical. When Christians say that Christ was " God of God, Light of Light, very God of very God " and

" of one substance with the Father," they are testifying that he who has brought redemption and new life to themselves and countless others must in some incomprehensible way have had God in him. They are asserting that God Himself has broken through the veil that separates man from Him and disclosed fully His nature as redemptive love in Jesus of Nazareth.

The *Christological doctrine* that Christ united in his person two natures, divine and human, was required to supplement the Nicene formulation of the Church's conviction about Christ's relation to God. Under the influence of the profound experiences of spiritual liberation and power we have described, there was a natural tendency of many early Christians to *deny the humanity* of Jesus or to absorb it into his divinity. Before the end of the first century there were " Docetists " who denied that the human nature, limitations and sufferings of Jesus could have been more than apparent or seeming. To simple piety it was natural to think of him simply as a God who appeared in the guise of a man rather than as the incarnation of God in a truly human being. Even responsible Greek theologians were tempted to deny or minimize the real humanity of Christ as a result of their dualistic philosophical assumptions about the nature of God and His relations to man. If God is conceived as immutable, infinite, and incapable of suffering, how can His nature be united with a human nature capable of growth, limited in knowledge and power, susceptible to suffering ? Some went so far as to say that his " rational soul," the centre of his personality, belonged not to his human nature but to the divine Word in him.

Fortunately, there were Christians who were more faithful to the portrait of the historical Jesus of the Gospels. These insisted that God had redeemed men by the incarnation of the Word in a *fully human* person, who grew in wisdom and stature, was tempted like ourselves and really suffered and died. It is the glory of the school of Christian thinkers at Antioch in the fourth and fifth centuries that in this way they strongly affirmed the humanity of Jesus. They conceived of the union of the divine and human nature in Christ as a union, not of " *nature* " or " *essence*," but of *will* and *purpose*. At every stage of his career he united his will and purpose with that of the indwelling Word. The response of the rational soul of Jesus to the leading of the indwelling Word was free. He could have sinned, but he was constant in his devotion to the Divine Will, in word and in deed, in life and in death. Thus, the unity of the human with the divine was brought about, not by the assumption of human " nature " by divine " nature," but by the spiritual influence of the Divine Word upon the human nature of Christ and the voluntary response of the latter to that influence. In short, the union of the divine and the human was not an abstract metaphysical one but a moral and spiritual one.

The weakness of this strikingly modern theory, it was felt by many, was that the unity of the personality of Christ was threatened by the strong insistence upon the *distinctness of the two natures* in him. It was also charged that it laid so much stress upon the exercise of the *human will* of Jesus in attaining unity with God that his divinity became little more than the quality or disposition of the will of a human being. Doubtless there is an element of truth in each of these criticisms, though the Antiochenes were as convinced as their Alexandrian opponents of the reality of the Incarnation and of the dependence of the moral will and purpose of Jesus upon the influence of the indwelling Word. On the other hand, while the Alexandrian theory had the value of stressing more strongly the divine factor in the person of Jesus, it tended to *confuse the human*

nature with the divine nature and virtually to swallow it
up in the latter.

The Council of Chalcedon in the fifth century
attempted both to safeguard the full *human nature of
Jesus* against the tendency to deny it and to assert
the *unity of his personality* against the tendency to
emphasize too strongly the distinctness of the divine
and human natures in him. It affirmed that Christ
was " of one essence with the Father as regards his
Godhead, and at the same time of one essence with
us as regards his manhood, in all respects like us,
apart from sin . . . proclaimed in two natures, without
confusion, without change, without division, without
separation." Obviously this does not solve the mystery
as to how two disparate " natures " can be united in
one " person," or how if they are united they can be
" without confusion " with one another. It merely
reasserts the conviction that the fullness of the divine
nature was in Christ, but insists also that he had a
fully human nature. It is an attempt to put into words
what cannot be put into words. For the paradox of
two different " natures " being brought together in
one person, so that they are neither confused nor
separated, strains logic to the breaking-point. The
Chalcedonian formula, accordingly, has been regarded
by more than one Christian theologian as the bank-
ruptcy of the whole Greek way of thinking about
Christ in terms of a sharp *dualism* between the divine
and human " natures." Its value is that it insists upon
both the divine and the human aspects of Christ and
at the same time upon the unity of his personality
without pretending to explain the paradox. But it is
not to be expected of any formula, stated in terms
derived from Greek dualistic ways of thinking about
God in *His separation from man,* that it should be
adequate to express the heart of the Christian experience
of Christ as *bringing God near to man.*

This suggests the *limitations* as well as the advantages of credal formulæ like those of Nicaea and Chalcedon. They should be taken as symbols of that in the nature of Christ and his relation to God which has been experienced by Christians but which cannot be adequately expressed in words or fully comprehended by reason. Since they are couched mainly in the language of prose, unimaginative Christians have tended to impute literal and exclusive truth to them. In this way, they have taken the central place in the religion of many, and blind conformity to them at every point has been demanded as the primary condition of membership in the Church. This has not only perverted their true meaning and purpose ; it has also repelled honest minds within and without the Church and led to a wholesale rejection of all creeds and all theologies. For this reason every age of Christianity must insist upon its right and its duty to interpret the essential truths preserved in the creeds according to the spirit rather than the letter. The assertion that Christ is " the likeness of the unseen God " has always been more important than the theory, orthodox or otherwise, by which men have tried to explain it. It is intelligible only in the light of the discovery by Christians through the centuries of the will and purpose of God in him as in no other man. As we shall see in the next section, this discovery about his *person* was at the same time a discovery about his *work* of redemption, the discovery that " God was in Christ reconciling the world to Himself."

VI.   THE ATONEMENT

THE affirmations of the Christian faith concerning revelation, God, and Christ, are all difficult for the modern rationalist because they interpret the deeper meaning of reality in terms of individual and unique events of history rather than abstract and universal ideas. The doctrine of the *Atonement*, or the *reconciliation* of man to God through the life and death of Christ, presents him with a further difficulty, for the traditional formulations of it seem to him either fantastic or immoral. He is unaware that the Church has not committed itself unreservedly to any of these formulations and he is often troubled because he cannot believe some theory which his own branch of the Church has found congenial and which he therefore assumes to be authoritative. It is well to make clear at the outset that the Church is committed only to the belief that Christ was crucified for the sins of men and that the Cross has the power to redeem those who see in it both the love of God and His condemnation of sin.

Why have Christians from the beginning found in the *crucifixion* a significance deeper than that of other events in the career of Jesus ? Why does the account of Passion Week occupy a third of the Gospel of Mark ? Why does St. Paul put " Christ crucified " in the centre of his preaching, " unto Jews a stumblingblock, and unto Gentiles foolishness, but unto them that are called, both Jews and Greeks, Christ the power of God, and the wisdom of God " ? (I Cor. 1 : 23–4). If Christians had seen in the crucifixion only the heroic death of a martyr for truth like Socrates, or the perfect expression of a human life devoted to the service of others, the modern rationalist or humanitarian might understand it more easily. Instead, they have spoken of a " ransom " of men from the power of the devil, or a " vicarious satisfaction " paid by an innocent man for the sins of the guilty. To the rationalist, the first of these ideas seems to be little more than a relic of primitive demonology, the second a reflection of a profoundly immoral conception of justice. Would it not be more intelligible to say simply that Christ's life provided an " example " for men and that his death was simply the culmination of his sacrificial life of love ?

On closer examination, however, it will be found that the earlier theories of the Atonement were groping efforts to express in the concepts that were available an experience of salvation which is not fully described in the modern " exemplarist " theories. Let us look briefly at two of these traditional theories, one of which was characteristic of the early and the other of the mediæval Church.

Behind the early view of the Atonement as a *ransom* freeing men from the devil there is much more than Semitic demonology. There is the conviction of generation after generation of Christians that somehow on the Cross the forces of evil met the power of God in mortal battle and were decisively beaten. The early Christians were vividly aware that by their faith in Christ they had been freed from the power of sin and the fear of death and that they had entered into a new life through the indwelling of his Spirit in them. The fact that they attributed the power of sin to demonic forces, and dramatized their liberation from it as a defeat of those invisible spiritual beings, is of secondary importance. The important thing is that a *victory* had been won over the source of all moral evils and the most fearful of all natural evils. God had shown His power in Christ and had put His enemies to flight. The Cross, viewed in this light, meant more than the suffering of a helpless *human victim*, it meant also the liberating power of a *Divine Victor* over sin and death. Moreover, with the defeat of sin and death, the Cross brought to the early Christians a new righteousness and a new life.

If we are to understand fully this view of the early Church, we must bear in mind that the whole public ministry of Jesus which culminated in the crucifixion

L

was marked by his *extraordinary power* over human lives. The emphasis of liberal Protestantism upon the selfless love of Jesus, as well as the stress of sentimental Catholicism upon his suffering, has blinded many Christians and others to the power of his personality. His healings to those who witnessed them seemed mighty and wonderful deeds, his teaching that of " one having authority." In short, the power of the historical Jesus to liberate men from disease and sin and bring them into a new life is written large on the whole Gospel record.

Moreover, the early Christians saw the Cross in the light of the *resurrection appearances*. The nature of these appearances will probably always remain a mystery. There is some evidence to indicate that they were spiritual rather than physical in character and that the story of the empty tomb may have arisen afterwards to account for them. Whatever their nature, it is certain that the disciples were convinced by them that the power of God which had confronted them in Jesus of Nazareth had not been destroyed by his death but had been released to work in their lives more effectively through the Holy Spirit. It was their sense of being possessed and strengthened by the Spirit which persuaded them that God had wrought a great victory through Christ on the Cross.

We must also bear in mind the ancient sense of the *unity* and *solidarity* of all humanity. Under the influence of the Hebraic tendency to think of the individual as part of the corporate life of the nation and the Platonic theory of the particular man as an example of universal humanity, the early Fathers had a strong sense of the solidarity of all men. This enabled them to see the reality of corporate evil more clearly than modern individualists are able to do. It also enabled them to think of the deliverance from evil and the attainment of eternal life for all humanity as having taken place, in principle, once and for all in Christ. As Adam represents all humanity in its sinful condition, they said, so Christ represents it as redeemed. His victory over sin and death is thus in anticipation the victory of all who accept him in faith and unite their lives with his. He is the founder of a new humanity, redeemed from evil and raised into newness of life.

It cannot be denied that, even when it is separated from the fantastic idea of a ransom paid to the devil, the view that on the Cross a victory over evil was won for all humanity seems foreign to our modern ways of thinking. One reason for this is that the Platonic notion of universal humanity runs counter to our deeper appreciation of individuality. But the permanent value of the theory can be stated in terms which are more meaningful to us. The early Christians were aware that, though the victory of Christ over evil had been won once and for all, it must be accepted by faith individually and must lead to a victory over evil in the life of each Christian. If they stressed the victory of Christ over evil as an objective and given event in the past, it was not because they overlooked the necessity of a personal struggle on the part of each of his followers with evil, but because they saw what a difference had actually been made in the life of humanity by that event. They saw that the power of God had made itself felt in history decisively in the life and death of Christ, that the Kingdom of God had drawn near in him and had already produced its first fruits in the lives of Christians. They saw that a new life for humanity had dawned, and that, though the powers of evil had not been finally vanquished, God through Christ had overcome them in principle. What was necessary now was only that the victorious Divine Power that had manifested itself in Christ should be received and allowed to have its way in their lives. If we are to put this into modern terms, we may say that in fact a *new kind of life* did come into history with Christ, that individuals and societies have been *raised to a higher level* when it has taken hold of them, and that the *redemptive power of God* is clearly to be seen throughout the process.

In a somewhat similar way, a profound truth may be found in the later view of Anselm that Christ through his death offered *satisfaction* to the honour of God in behalf of sinful humanity.[1] The positive value of this theory does not depend upon the terms in which it is stated, terms borrowed from the mediæval penitential system. It reminds us that sin must be taken seriously and that a holy God cannot tolerate it in His children who are to live in fellowship with Him. Of course, God is willing to forgive the sinner if he will only repent. But this must not become an excuse for sinful men to rest easy in their moral complacency. For true repentance involves much more than shame over being found out or disgust with oneself or occasional feelings of sorrow or even reso-

---

[1] The obvious weakness of this theory lies in the suggestion that God's *honour*, affronted by sin, had to be satisfied before His *mercy* could be bestowed upon sinners in forgiveness. This seems to imply a jealous concern of God for His own honour, a concern which binds him to the law that His honour must be satisfied and thus prevents His love from being bestowed freely upon men. At the same time, it represents *Christ* as willingly enduring death and thus seems to contrast his mercy and love with the stern justice of the *Father*. The result has sometimes been to arouse grateful love to the Son, but at the same time awful fear toward the Father. It is probable, however, that Anselm did not mean to assert such a dualism between justice and mercy in the Godhead, or between the honour of the Father and the love of the Son, since the Father Himself initiates the process by which His honour is satisfied.

It must also be admitted that Anselm's theory of sin as the withholding of a debt due to God which must be compensated for by an equivalent payment is unfortunate. But his statement that it was not " fitting " for God to pass over sin as if there were no difference between the guilty and the innocent, and that if He had done so he would have acted in an arbitrary way " subject to no law," gives a clue to his real meaning. When it is objected by the enquiring believer that " a single repentant feeling on my part would blot out this sin," Anselm replies soberly : " You have not yet estimated the great burden of sin." (*Cur Deus Homo*, Bk. I, Ch. XXI).

The theory of Calvin that the death of Christ was a *substitutionary penalty* for the sins of men and that it was necessary to appease the wrath of God represents a hardening of this profound insight. It is rightly rejected by modern Christians both because it is foreign to the New Testament idea of God to think of Him as needing to be appeased and because it is meaningless to speak of a penalty being imposed upon a sinless man.

lutions to do better. It implies a radical break with
self-centredness and a determination to face about and
devote oneself completely to God's will. And part
of the difficulty is that sinful men are not able to
repent unless something is done to break the hold of
egoism upon them. Unless real repentance occurs
forgiveness would be futile, for it would lead to no
real change in man's relation to God, his character,
or his attitude toward his fellows.

According to the Christian view, forgiveness is
possible because the moral law is not an inflexible
principle but instrumental to the divine providence.
But this does not mean, as sentimental humanitarians
often assume, that the justice of God can be set aside
as if it were of no account, or that the love of God
can accept sinful men as if they were not sinful. It
is not that an angry God has to be propitiated or
appeased by a blood sacrifice before He is willing to
forgive ; it is that He must make what St. Paul called
a " demonstration of His righteousness " and of its
radical opposition to sin if His forgiveness is to be
morally significant. Christians have always seen in
the Cross such a demonstration against sin. There
the sins of men, of all the Pharisees, high priests,
Pilates, and howling mobs of history, stand condemned
in the most dramatic way, since they brought the only
sinless man to a shameful death.

Moreover, the rejection of mediæval or Reformation
theories of a *vicarious satisfaction* or *penalty* should not
blind us to the redemptive value of the *vicarious
suffering* of Christ and those who have his spirit.
Modern individualists, in their devotion to the principle of moral autonomy, are especially in need of
this warning. From the days of St. Paul, Christians
have always seen in the Cross a demonstration of the
costliness of the divine love for men and have felt its
power to redeem their lives through the response of

gratitude and love it awakens in them. In the face of this historical fact, the idea of individualists that vicarious suffering is immoral is petty. Moreover the vicarious suffering of Christ has an analogy in countless lives of sacrificial love which have had redemptive power over others. Such lives help us to understand the words of the prophet of the Exile : " He was wounded for our transgressions, he was bruised for our iniquities ; the chastisement of our peace was upon him ; and with his stripes we are healed " (Is. 53 : 5).

We have emphasized the elements of truth in the traditional " objective " theories of the Atonement because they have been overlooked by many modern Christians. But the " *moral influence* " views also call attention to an important truth. Every theory of the Atonement which stops with the assertion of what God did *for* man in Christ and does not go on to show how what He did works its benefits *in* men is amoral. As Christ died and rose again, says St. Paul, the Christian must die to sin in the flesh and rise to newness of life in the Spirit. Therefore he glories that *he* can " die daily " and fill out the measure of Christ's sufferings. This is the fundamental truth that the " moral influence " theory of Abélard and others seeks to express. The redemption of man from sin and death by the love of Christ on the Cross has meaning for the Christian only as it arouses gratitude and enkindles love in his heart. Moreover, the death of Christ must not be isolated from his life as a whole and the incarnation treated as important only as leading to the crucifixion. Christ redeems men by his teachings and his life as well as by his death.

The full meaning of this theory is lost if it is interpreted in a narrow moralistic sense. According to Abélard, Christ provides a pattern or example for men's lives by his deeds and his teachings. But Abélard also recognizes that men must have moral incentive and power to do what is right. The Law had confronted them with commandments but had not given the ability to fulfil them. At the best, men were able to obey these commandments in their external conduct from the motive of fear. But an act is morally good only if its *intention* is good. It was necessary, therefore, that God should not only reveal the *pattern of goodness* but also arouse that love for Himself which creates the *desire for goodness*. As the manifestation of God's love, Christ awakened in men this new motive of love, and thus taught them to do his will, voluntarily as sons rather than fearfully as slaves.

Moreover, this theory is not to be interpreted in a purely " subjective " sense, as has often been done. In the highest human love, the lover identifies himself with the one loved and brings about a transformation in him through his response to the moral influence brought to bear upon him. So God in the sufferings and death of Christ " identifies Himself in sympathy with the sins and sufferings of His human children— and through the revelation of His self-sacrificing love calls forth on their part that corresponding love for Him which makes possible their forgiveness and ultimate restoration."[1] Conceived in this way, the " moral influence " theory is far from being purely " subjective," since it represents God as taking the initiative in reconciling men to Himself as an " objective " historical fact. Thus, it does not exclude the elements of truth in the " objective " theories we have already described, but emphasizes the way in which the redemptive love of God manifested in the historical Jesus awakens a response in his followers and thus becomes a transforming power in their lives. The truth is, all three of the theories we have described

---

[1] W. A. Brown, article, " Expiation and Atonement," in Hastings' *Encyclopedia of Religion and Ethics*, Vol. V.

are needed if we are to do justice to different sides of the work of Christ. The life and death of Christ has brought to men victory over sin and newness of life ; it has demonstrated the appalling depth of sin and God's condemnation of it ; and it has stimulated men to a self-sacrificing love like that of Christ.

VII. SALVATION BY FAITH AND NEW LIFE IN THE SPIRIT

OPPOSED to the humanistic idea that we can *save ourselves* by our own reason, moral efforts, social reforms, scientific discoveries, cultural achievements, and economic and political efforts is the Christian affirmation that we are saved *by God* through *faith*. This is the meaning of St. Paul's teaching, revived with such vigour by Luther, that we are " justified " by faith and faith alone. Justification by faith rather than good works is based upon the simple, realistic recognition of our egoistic pride and selfishness, the misery we bring upon ourselves and others by our sin, and our powerlessness to overcome it by ourselves. To modern humanists and romanticists, deluded by optimistic views of the natural goodness and rationality of man, this has seemed a mere confession of weakness, if not a counsel of despair. In a sense, of course, it is ; and as Professor Greene has said, it can have no meaning to anyone who is conscious of no sense of deep need and failure in himself. But it rests also upon the belief that the sin and misery of man are in contradiction to his true nature and that God in His benevolent purpose wills to redeem man from his bondage to evil and to restore him to his dignity as a spiritual being.

Thus faith in the grace and mercy of God in Christ brings about a *reconciliation* with Him as the Source of existence and value. It is the beginning of a new life in the Spirit, a *regeneration* of life. For salvation requires not only faith in the divine grace as mercy, but also

surrender to the divine grace as transforming power.
Regeneration brings about the liberation of the self
from its paralyzing egoism into creative and self-giving
life.   It restores the self to its true spiritual nature
and bestows upon it the peace and joy that come with
health.

St. Paul speaks of the new life of the Christian as
lived " *in the spirit* " rather than the " *flesh*."   This
has sometimes been misunderstood.   It does not mean
primarily mastery by the reason, conceived as the
higher self, over the lower self of animal appetite.
This is the doctrine of Platonic dualism, not Christianity.
St. Paul's emphasis is upon possession of the human
spirit by the Spirit that was in Christ as the source of
a new life raised above the level of natural human
existence.   In the Fourth Gospel, Jesus is represented
as saying, " That which is born of the flesh is flesh :
and that which is born of the Spirit is spirit " (John 3 : 6).
Clearly, this way of thinking about a rebirth " from
above " is to be understood, not primarily in terms of
the Platonic dualism between rational and irrational
parts of the soul, but in terms of the Old Testament
idea of the Divine Spirit which inspires or indwells
the spirit of the prophet.   Thus, life " in the spirit "
means more than the " life of reason " :   it is an
" inspired " life, a life controlled " from above " by the
Spirit of Christ or the Holy Spirit.

The remarkable thing about the Christian view of
the regenerate life is that it is meant to apply to *every*
Christian.   In the book of Acts the story of the coming
of the Holy Spirit at Pentecost upon all the assembly
illustrates this point, and St. Paul always takes it for
granted in his epistles.   The early Christian community
lived constantly, as it were, in the atmosphere of the
supernatural.   The very heart of the Christian life was
the experience of being strengthened, guided, unified,
and perfected by the Spirit.

The established Churches have tended to forget this or even to be afraid of it because of the excesses of " enthusiasm " and " subjectivism " to which it sometimes leads. They have preferred to think of guidance by the Spirit as indirect, mediated by the Church and its priests, and in harmony with orthodox dogma. They have assumed that Jesus' promise to the disciples in the Fourth Gospel,[1] " when he, the Spirit of truth, is come, he will guide you into all truth," was not a promise of new truth but only of a better understanding of the old. But from time to time throughout its history the Church has been stirred by movements or " sects " based on the ideal of a community of true believers living by the Spirit rather than a lifeless body of conventional and uninspired persons. Sometimes the leaders of these movements have separated themselves at the outset from the established Churches and founded small Christian groups, as in the case of the Society of Friends. Sometimes, like John Wesley, they have attempted to reform the established Churches from within by converting " almost " into " altogether " Christians through a personal experience of " heartfelt " religion. The established Churches themselves owe more than they usually acknowledge to these movements.

Thus, reconciliation with God through faith involves a regeneration or transformation of life by the indwelling of the Holy Spirit. Its moral fruit is the *passion for perfect goodness*. If Christians believe that man can never *achieve* perfect goodness by his own will alone, even when he has a revealed Law to guide his conscience, they also take for granted that perfect goodness is the *goal* of moral striving and that a holy God can have complete fellowship only with those who " hunger and thirst " after it.

It is the fashion in certain Neo-Orthodox circles to

[1] John 16: 13.

scoff at the " *perfectionism* " of some Christians.   The
regenerate man, we are told, must continue to struggle
to the end with the remnants of sin in his life.   The
ethic of Jesus is admitted in these circles to be a
" perfectionist " ethic, based upon absolute obedience
to the will of God interpreted in terms of the law of
love.   But the power of sin prevents this ethic of love
from ever being practised fully by individuals or more
than distantly approximated by social groups.

This is a valuable corrective of modern sentimental
views of the natural man's moral capacity.   But it is
difficult to see how it can without qualification be
rendered consistent with Jesus' injunction, " You must
be merciful as your heavenly Father is merciful," with
his warning, " I tell you, unless your goodness excels
that of the scribes and Pharisees, you will never get
into the Realm of Heaven," and with the heroic spirit
of his teaching as a whole.   Nor is it true to the teaching
of St. Paul, who assumes that the believer who is " in
Christ " must seek to expel all sin from his life.   Absolute
perfection in this life, of course, must not be claimed
for any Christian, however saintly.   It is strenuous
effort and progress toward perfection that St. Paul
asserts of himself, and it is better to speak in relative
rather than absolute terms.   Christian perfection, in
short, is a " regulative ideal," not an actual fact.
What is essential is not that perfection shall be fully
attainable in this life, but that no goal below it should
ever be accepted as adequate by the Christian and
that no limits should ever be put upon the power of
the Spirit of God to transform his life.

The ideal of perfection has been discredited in the
eyes of many, not only by the sentimental optimism
and the self-righteousness of some of its defenders, but
also by the *legalistic conception* of it as literal obedience
to the " commandments " of God in the Old Testament
and the " precepts " of Christ in the New.   Puritanism

was at times guilty of this legalistic view of goodness and Protestant groups have been influenced by it in their insistence upon abstinence from many acts of doubtful moral significance, e.g., theatregoing and cardplaying. The answer to this misconception is that Christian perfection should be defined in terms of a religious rather than a legalistic morality. It is rooted in the religious experience of communion with God in faith and love. This religious experience gives rise spontaneously to an outgoing love of neighbour. Thus, the essence of Christian perfection is, not literal obedience to revealed commandments in external conduct, but pure and unselfish love manifesting itself in ways suitable to the ever-new and ever-changing situations of human life.

The Roman Catholic Church has emphasized the *contemplative* aspect of perfection, the " vision of God," partly because of the conviction that worship is the heart of religion, partly under the influence of Greek intellectualism and mediæval monasticism. The Protestant Churches, on the other hand, have stressed the *active*, *moral* element, sometimes sacrificing worship to conduct. The Evangelicals have put *love* and the social expression of love in service in the foreground of their ideal. But whenever one aspect of perfection is stressed at the expense of the others, there is sure to be a reaction. For perfection is the fulfilment of *all* sides of human nature, contemplative and active and emotional, individual and social. Human nature as part of the Creation is regarded by the Christian as good, and *all* the faculties must be regarded as " talents " or " gifts " to be developed and used in the service of God.

The need for a recovery of this ideal of personality is shown by even a cursory survey of the moral and cultural standards of contemporary life. The loss of the ideal of Christian perfection as the crown of a

Spirit-possessed life is symbolized by the virtual dis-
appearance of the term " saint " from our vocabulary.
The result has been a serious weakening of the spiritual
life in all its phases. The dominant ideal of character
in recent generations has been that of the congenial,
sociable, adjusted person who pleases everyone but
lacks moral principles and spiritual depth. In a
similar fashion, the loss of the passion for perfection
has much to do with the shallowness of our culture.
A deep love of philosophic wisdom and of beauty (as
distinguished from mere sensuous charm) is almost as
rare as a deep love of God and love of goodness. As
a result, the vital energies of our people are far too
largely spent upon sexual excitement, economic acqui-
sition, and meaningless social activities. This *degradation
of personality* can be overcome only by the process we
have just described : *reconciliation* with God through
faith, *regeneration* of the self by His indwelling Spirit,
and unremitting effort to approximate more nearly
the goal of *perfect goodness* in love.

VIII. THE KINGDOM OF GOD, HISTORY AND COMMUNITY

To stop at this point, however, would be to limit
Christian salvation to *persons*, as if *society* and its
institutions were beyond redemption. Almost from the
outset, the genius of the Christian movement has been
otherwise. Christians rejoiced in their fellowship within
the Church ; but they regarded the Church as only
the " first fruits " of the Kingdom of God. It is true
that for some time the early Christians accepted the
existing social institutions, making no attempt to overthrow slavery, the economic order, or the Empire.
But as they increased in numbers and influence, as
they came to realize that the " second coming " of
Christ was indefinitely remote, and as they began to
see the social implications of their faith, this attitude

was modified. From the beginning there had been a gradual transformation of institutions such as the family and the school. From the third century perfectionistic monks began to withdraw from the corrupt, worldly life of society and to establish monastic communities in which they could realize the Christian life without compromise. Others stayed within the world, and, while they rationalized their own compromise with its economic injustice and political oppression, idealized the monastic life of poverty and brotherhood. More daring reformers and sects in the mediæval period sought to recall the Church and their fellow-Christians to the simplicity and otherworldliness of New Testament times. The result was a gradual transformation of social institutions from within, despite the prevailing conservatism.

In the modern period of rapid change a more *radical interpretation* of the social implications of the Gospel has arisen. The justification for this radical social Christianity is to be found, first, in the *ethical teaching* of Jesus. As is well known, there is very little explicitly social teaching in the Gospels. The family is the only social institution about which Jesus says anything specific. His teaching about true greatness—" whosoever would be first among you, shall be servant of all " (Mk. 10 : 44)—and his distinction between " the things that are Caesar's " and " the things that are God's " have political implications. And his numerous sayings about wealth cannot be reconciled with the acquisitive spirit, with callous indifference to the needs of the poor, and with neglect of the spiritual life. But it is the teaching of Jesus about *love of neighbour*, exemplified by his own concern for the healing of men's bodies as well as their souls, that has had the most significant effect. When it is once grasped that love of neighbour is more than a feeling, that it is a settled disposition to further the welfare of persons, and that it is bestowed especially upon the poor and the undeserving, the Social Gospel is not far off.

A second justification for radical social Christianity is to be found in Jesus' teaching about the *Kingdom of God*. Jesus was heir to centuries of Jewish Messianic speculation, the central idea of which was the future establishment of the Reign or Kingdom of God in the lives of men. This hope is one of the most revealing expressions of Hebrew prophetic teaching about God's purpose in history. It cannot be understood unless one bears in mind what has already been said about the Hebraic conception of God and His moral purpose for men. If God is good and if He is the Lord of history, it follows that evil must ultimately be defeated and good must triumph by His intervention. Whether the divine intervention would be direct or mediated by a Messiah, whether the Kingdom would be established on earth, in heaven, or upon a renovated and transfigured earth, whether it would include righteous Gentiles as well as Jews—these and other questions admitted of different answers. The one essential thing was that God would overthrow the demonic and human powers of evil and set up a kingdom of justice, peace, and joy.

This Kingdom was always conceived by the prophets as a *community*. To Jews, with their keen awareness of the importance of corporate life, no other conception would have been possible. And, though Jesus held that men must render personal obedience to God, metaphors such as that of the Messianic feast show the social character of the Kingdom for him. Moreover, the Kingdom in the teaching of Jesus is an *ideal, spiritual* community, for which a man should be willing to sacrifice all earthly possessions, break all earthly ties, even those of the family, and take up the Cross itself to attain its blessedness. This, together with the ethic of love which is closely related to it, is the source of

the radical social implications of the Gospel. Apparently
indifferent to the form of social institutions and to the
earthly interests served by them, it holds before men's
eyes a vision of an ideal and inclusive community of
love. Put in the balance with such a community, the
institutions and interests of every human society are
weighed and found wanting. At most they have a
relative value ; and wherever they conflict with the
absolute ends of the Kingdom they must be transformed.

Moreover, the *movement of history* as a whole is to be
seen in the light of the Kingdom as its supreme goal.
Christ, as the Founder of the ideal community, the
perfect embodiment of its new life, and the Head of
the Church which is its " first fruits," is the centre of
history, dividing the old, which finds in him the fulfilment of its gropings, from the new which looks back to
him for its inspiration and guidance. For the Christian
life is not merely faith in Christ as personal Saviour,
it is also faith in the Kingdom of God as the goal of
history and active participation in the movement of
history toward that goal. The Christian looks back
to Christ as the incarnation of God's redemptive purpose ; but he also looks forward to the fulfilment of
that redemptive purpose in the future. This provides
a powerful sanction for both the personal acceptance
and the social application of the Gospel.

Will the Kingdom of God be realized *within the
limits of history* or *beyond history in a heavenly state ?* It
is generally agreed by modern New Testament scholars
that Jesus conceived of the Kingdom as a future state
that was to be ushered in by a Last Judgment in which
the righteous would be separated from the unrighteous.
In so far as the present era is in bondage to the powers
of evil, it must be destroyed. As a result, many
Christians have drawn pessimistic conclusions about
earthly existence in time and have regarded the Kingdom exclusively as a future heavenly state. This life

was only a pilgrimage toward the " Heavenly City."
The proper attitude of the Christian toward its interests
and pleasures was one of detachment ; and there was
no hope of social progress through reform, much less
of an approximation to the Kingdom of God in the
" earthly city." Protestant orthodoxy has sought to
justify this otherworldly view of the Kingdom by an
almost exclusive emphasis upon sin in its doctrine of
man.

But a more hopeful view of the *possibilities of history*
is defended by modern Christians. They can point to
evidence that for Jesus the Kingdom of God was not
only a future hope but a *present reality*. " The Kingdom
of God is among [or within] you " is only one of his
sayings which indicate that the divine power was already
showing itself. The parables of growth, e.g., the sower
and the seed growing of itself, are most naturally interpreted as indicating a process that had already begun.
Jesus seems to have regarded his healing power and his
moral effect upon the lives of others as indicating that
Satan and his demons were already being put to flight.
Certainly, the experience of his followers after the Holy
Spirit had fallen upon them at Pentecost was that they
were already living in the beginnings of the new order.
They looked forward to the second coming of the
Master to establish the Kingdom in its fullness, but
they already had a foretaste of its joys and were showing
its " first fruits " in their lives. Moreover, Jesus
stressed the necessity of *preparation* for the coming of
the Kingdom. There were conditions of entrance into
the Kingdom which must be met here and now. The
day and hour of the consummation no man knew,
not even himself ; that could be left in the hands of
God (Mk. 13 : 32). Meanwhile, the sower would sow
his seed in the knowledge that some would receive it
and a harvest would be reaped.

His followers have done, and must continue to do,

M

the same. Except for the millenarians who lose themselves in dreams and visions of an earthly Kingdom of
Christ, Christians do not make predictions about the
earthly future. They do not accept the naïve modern
beliefs in inevitable progress or the social utopianism
that accompanies it. They put their final hopes, not
on time, but on eternity. They know that the hope
for *eternal life* after death cannot be proved by reason.
But in some form it seems to them to be required by
what they know about the human spirit, by the worth
of human personality, and by the love of God for His
children. Even in the midst of time, they feel that
eternal life is theirs ; they can live for eternity here
and now, because they have passed from death to life.
Thus, they are not tempted to stake all their hopes on
temporal goods or make exaggerated claims for the
possibilities of history.

But the hope of eternal life does not prevent Christians
from seeking to *approximate the Kingdom in history* as far
as their weakness and that of their fellows will permit.
Indeed, it gives them a strong incentive to do so, for
it puts their earthly efforts in a wider setting and enables
them to see the eternal significance of that which they
do in time. Unless time and eternity are radically
opposed to one another as in Platonic dualism—an
opposition which is inconsistent with the Christian
belief in a God of history—eternity must fulfil that
which time has begun. Christians know, therefore,
that their efforts to approximate the Kingdom of God
by radically transforming social institutions and relationships will not be in vain. They know that the first
task of the Church is the regeneration of individuals.
But they are convinced that the redemptive purpose of
God also extends to communities and that true community must be based upon Christian love and
brotherhood.

Thus, the answer of Christianity to the *need of modern*

society for unity is fundamentally identical with its answer to the need of modern individuals for a centre of meaning : reconciliation with God through faith and transformation by the love which was in Christ. For *love* which flows from faith is the deepest source of unity within the community, qualifying the liberty of the individual by his responsibility to others. This way of thinking about community is neither identical with Aristotle's dictum that man is a " political animal," nor with the modern sociologist's doctrine that man is a " social being." According to the Christian view, man is social, not only by virtue of his membership in a particular society, but also by virtue of his sonship to God and his membership in the family of God. Nature and history bind him to his fellows by ties of blood, need, reciprocity, language, and tradition. But over and above all such bonds is the bond of his membership in the potentially *universal community* of those who seek to serve God by loving their neighbours. There cannot be a full realization of this ideal community among the kingdoms of this world, for all the forces of self-love are arrayed against it. But those whose faith is in it as the goal of history must seek wherever they are a kind of community which will reflect the perfect love of the Kingdom in good will, justice and peace.

In conclusion, it should be emphasized that the Christian faith is an *organic unity*. Its central affirmations may be distinguished from one another for purposes of analysis, as has been done in this chapter. But they are interdependent and inseparably united in the experience of the Christian. Thus, the Christian conception of God is at once presupposed and completed by the conception of Christ and the Atonement made possible by him, while this in turn assumes the Christian understanding of man's Sin and his need of Salvation.

It also needs to be said that the *intellectual interpretation* of the Christian faith, though important, is *secondary to the Christian experience* and must be understood in the light of that experience. Besides, the value of any such interpretation is of necessity limited by the experience, insight, and power of expression of the Christian thinker. It should be regarded simply as a statement of the meaning of the faith to a particular Christian. Since it will differ in some measures from the interpretation of any other Christian thinker, assent to it by other Christians should never be insisted upon. Rather, it should be offered with deep humility and full recognition that depths of mystery have not yet been plumbed. Though " the reason of man is the candle of the Lord, lighted by God and lighting man to God," it is often a feeble and flickering candle.

Finally, the Christian faith is not a system of beliefs which only a philosopher or theologian can understand. Though the Gospel may require subtle and prolonged thinking to make clear its full meaning and implications, its essence is *simple*. The uneducated worker can understand it as well as the educated theologian ; and, though he may not be as able to expound its meaning in words, he may express it more fully in deeds. Its essence is Christ and the new life he brought into the world, and difficulties of interpretation ought never to prevent anyone from committing himself in faith to it.

But it is as *profound* as it is simple. The wise and the successful need it no less than the simple and the weak, though it may be harder for them in their pride to see or admit their need. That is why we must return to the Christian faith, in its simplicity *and* its profundity, if we are to attain fullness and wholeness in our lives and establish justice and peace in our world.

IV

CHRISTIANITY AND SOCIETY

EDWIN E. AUBREY

THE opening chapter presented four challenges to Christian thought on the social problem of our generation. Let us now see how Christianity can meet these challenges with the resources provided for us in the two chapters immediately preceding. We shall not repeat the philosophical and theological arguments set forth in these two chapters but shall try to show their *social* bearings. From Dr. Tillich's massive indictment of contemporary culture we may raise into relief four key words : security, unity, freedom, and significance.

I. SECURITY

WITH war of unparalleled destruction dragging into its ninth year, men are asking whether there is to be no security in international life from wanton aggression and chaotic nationalism. Conscious that for good or ill an economic order is passing off the scene, they are perplexed and anxious whether the new order will give a basis for a broader security for themselves and their families against want. Confronted by a new threat of racial strife, the extent and terror of which cannot now be gauged, they fear for the safety of their own race, but remain bewildered as to the nature of a genuine brotherhood of man in which the white minority must find its just place. The very magnitude of these revolutionary changes in the basis of living exerts a psychological pressure on the sensitive person, so that he is filled with a vague dread of personal insecurity, fearful that he cannot cope with the personal demands of the situation, and that his own inner life may go to pieces. Because we are all members of groups which are caught in the maelstrom of the present social revolution, we are all insecure. Hence we need to know what sort of security is possible for us.

The Christian answer to this demand for security is four-fold. First, there is no security without *realism*. A flight from reality is not security but insanity. It is insane to seek national security in isolation while the life of the world of which we are inextricably a part is being more and more unified through air power, interdependent economy, and cultural exchange. What society can hope to find real security in a past that is forever dead ? Or what individual can expect to achieve personal security in a chaotic social situation save in the realm of imagination ? The insistence on being realistic is grounded in the belief that the universe is really a unity and that this unity has a central meaning. For the attempt to deal with the realities is futile unless there is some integral connection between them and the immediate decision that must be made. Such an attempt implies that the world has unity and meaning, and is neither a mere illusion nor an unrelated welter of events. When a man tries to be realistic he is reckoning with all the facts that seem to be relevant to his decision ; but if there is no such thing as relevance then realism is meaningless.

In saying this we are affirming two fundamental articles of Christian faith : that God gives unity and meaning to the multifarious events of our world, and that this unity is dynamic rather than static. Therefore the Christian speaks of divine purpose, using the analogy of human purpose to describe the way in which many events enter into some single event in a time sequence. When a man executes a purpose he

combines a number of items found at successive stages
in his planning into the actual achievement of his goal.
For a purpose is more than a string of incidents along
the line from past to future. It is informed throughout
by some end or goal which lies beyond. If we enlarge
this to take in all of human history, then we shall
have to state that the purpose of God is always beyond
history even though it operates within history.

The demand for realism in social thought requires
us therefore to reckon with the complex social factors
in terms of the meaning of history. Otherwise we
have no criteria that can be applied in a world that
is forever moving beyond the present into the future.
Surely that man alone is realistic who sees the present
in terms of its future effects. Some philosophy of
history is inescapable for the realist.

If history has any unitary meaning, then this meaning
must be expressed more fully at some points than
others ; and the task of the realist is to locate those
points. But how can they be identified unless he
proceeds with some conception of what that meaning
is ? Amid the welter of contemporary international
events, contradictory economic tendencies, or rival
theories of education, how can he choose unless he
has some basis for judging relative values ? But
sound values must also be realistic : they must conform
to what is most real in the long run. But " what is
most real in the long run " is an abstract way of
referring to what " God " means. Hence the realistic
quest is a search for God.

But God must be found in history if He is to be
relevant to social thought. The Christian finds God
in history, as does the Jew, but the Christian declares
further that the meaning of God in history is distinc-
tively and supremely set forth in Jesus of Nazareth.
Therefore, from the standpoint of meaning, Jesus
Christ is the centre of history ; in him the divine

purpose for human life is objectively expressed. If we
want to know what God means concretely for human
history, there in Jesus is our answer. This assertion
is a mere shibboleth until we give definite content to
our notion of Jesus Christ ; but if he is really the
centre of meaning in a process of history that is continually transcending its successive presents, then our
notion of Jesus Christ cannot be exhaustive either.
Thus the Christian has confidence, but not complete
rational assurance. His realism includes acknowledgment of his own limitations ; and he cannot, so long
as he remains really Christian, ascribe absolute truth
to any of his own interpretations of Christ.

How, then, can he be realistically secure in the
world ? First of all, he can find relief from the chaos
which paralyzes thought and action by accepting some
specific belief as a basis for action. Then he has the
security which accompanies ability to act. But in
Christian faith he has more than this, for he is committed
to God as the ultimate meaning of things made known
to men in Jesus Christ. This ultimate meaning appears
in the guise of a humble, loving and suffering servant
of men, who so far transcends the conditions of his
career that he transfigures human life, taking up into
himself the sins of men and overcoming them by the
power of God's purpose.

What does this say about our realistic security ?
It says that humility and not pride is the clue to social
security, for pride is detached and exploitative, and
breaks down unity while humility is receptive and
builds connections with the lives of others. (Where
now is pride of race or nation ?) It says that love is
a better basis for community than mere justice.
Justice seeks a balancing of the interests within a
group but tends always to fall into a legalism in which
the interests are defined once for all, while love is
perpetually seeking to discover the growing interests

in the lives of growing persons and to anticipate them.
(Where now is the legalism which is the curse of
diplomacy and the persistent barrier to redistribution
of power and rights in the international scene ?)   It
says, further, that because men turn away in selfishness
and pride from the demands of love, the Christian way
is fraught with suffering and sacrifice, for the reconciling
act cannot be performed in a corrupt world without
inviting danger to oneself and one's group.

This is the terrible demand of Christ, and men rise
in protest against the " foolishness " of it.   The only
alternative is a struggle to wrest from the favoured
few that which the many need ; and the result of this
is domestic bloody revolution, or international war, or
an incalculable global conflict among the races of the
earth.   In this bloodiest of all the centuries of human
history we surely cannot pride ourselves on the realism
of our secular political thinking !   Why should we not
consider the realism of Christian thought ?

However, with this terrible demand of Christ there
comes a great promise.   Those who pay this cost find
God, the ultimately real, and therefore the true basis
of all human life.   Having found him they have the
deepest possible security.   This may be interpreted to
mean that the individual finds peace in the midst of
social strife—but not for long if he be socially sensitive.
It also means that social life can be rendered secure
through alliance with God as made known in Jesus Christ.
If God be the God of nature too, then the foundations
in nature for human society—the perennial golden
fleece of the sociologists—are also provided.   Science
can serve to explicate the details of this.   And since
God is God of all history, human security is not based
merely on the confidence of some particular age.   This
is the answer to Dr. Tillich's demand for a Christian
solution that transcends the prejudices of a bourgeois
epoch in Western culture.   God is not bound by

culture or by epoch. We must therefore act in our time and place by acting on a faith that goes beyond any given culture or any historical epoch. The Kingdom of God is not a Roman Empire, nor a feudal order, nor a bourgeois society, nor a Communist régime. It stands beyond them all and judges them, but it also points a way.

If the first condition of security is realism of the kind just discussed, the second condition is that security must be accompanied by *growth*. Provisions for amending the Constitution are part of our security under it. The Bill of Rights was the first bit of growing that our Constitution underwent. Enough men were sufficiently realistic to see that neither freedom, nor brotherhood, nor equality could be assured without these amendments. Similarly any organization for international security must carry its own provisions for growth as conditions require. To many the changes denote decay rather than growth. How, then, is change to be creative? Change may be purely destructive and lead to chaos; or it may contain the seeds of new order and spell creative advance. Security without growth may spell mediocrity. The exponents of a competitive economic system fear that loss of competition would mean stagnation, and if they are right, then surely the security of a planned economy would be false, for it would not allow for the growth that comes from vigorous effort. Whether economic vigour is guaranteed only by competition is a very different question; and besides, economic competition tends toward monopoly, which is the end of competition unless some form of planning controls the trusts. In another realm, security is often sought through government control so rigid as to deprive the person of significant freedom and decision, and hence of growth. This reduces the person to a mere integer, and distinctive personality is lost. The economic parallel is found in a mass-production system which mechanizes the worker. If the world and personality are both subject to the fact of change, then security can only be achieved by growth. This is the fundamental principle which invalidates conservative reaction. The reactionary can expect to be vindicated only when his turn comes around again in a world which is going in cycles. But Christianity specifically denies that we live in such a world.

Deeply rooted in the Judæo-Christian view of life is a dynamic interpretation of history that is unique among the philosophies of the world. History is not a vast illusion without value or meaning; nor is it a repetitious cyclical process always coming back on itself like the stars in their orbits. It is a meeting ground of divine purpose and human freedom; and its character is unintelligible apart from the struggles of men to evade that purpose even while they are free to accept it. One of the most startling aspects of the Bible is its willingness to attribute change to God Himself. Readers steeped in Greek philosophical absolutism have ascribed this to the primitive quality of Hebrew thinking. On the contrary it is a profounder understanding of God, and one to which recent philosophy is returning.

The changelessness of God is not an immutability in which nothing new emerges, but a steadiness of aim, an unchanging direction characterized by the determination to save men from themselves. This is the basis of biblical history; and it allows for changes in the divine way of acting, often indeed for radical changes, so that the biblical writer may even speak of God repenting. The perpetual intention of God to save mankind may require tender persuasion (" Come and let us reason together ") or terrible punishment (" I will scatter them as the stubble that passeth away "), according to the historical circumstances, in order to bring the people back within His purpose for them. Growth is essential to the very idea ; and thus the solution of the social problem must provide for growth too. Security without growth is only a temporary security.

The third condition of security is *fellowship*. No form of insecurity is psychologically more acute than that of not " belonging." The man without a country, the orphan without a family, the stranger in a far country among an alien race, the boy " sent to Coventry " by his schoolmates—these are insecure indeed. Intellectually this is expressed in the lack of conviction we experience when we can find no one to share our opinions. Then we fear for our own mental security. Again, a disrupted family can destroy a child's security, and an unstable economic order can undermine the personal security of the worker and the capitalist alike. There is little security without company. Since an individual is a person only in a social context, the security of his personality is contingent upon group life.

But security in a given age may be strengthened, or insecurity compensated, by fellowship with people of other ages. How often the lonely man has found new confidence through contact with great souls of other generations, with philosophers like Plato, or with reformers like Luther, or with saints like Francis of Assisi ! This fact is recognized by Christian thought in its doctrine of the Church, which has been summarized in the preceding chapter. The Church is a fellowship of many centuries and climates, many races and classes and countries, where the common bond is loyalty to Christ. His spirit and power invest the Church with strength not all its own. In this body of believers is security, and the individual is undergirded for severe struggles so that he rises to heights of courage and insight he could not attain alone. Witness the heroism of the European Churches under the Nazi heel. Just what this power is remains a sociological puzzle, for there is an element of the eternal in it that sociological categories do not encompass. " God is in the midst of her."

The Christian believes that this divine power is the power of the Holy Spirit. In efforts to formulate a doctrine of the Holy Spirit theologians have combined three great insights : that the bond of social unity is one with the bond of cosmic unity, of the unity of God Himself ; that this bond is love as set forth in the thirteenth chapter of Paul's first letter to the Corinthians ; and that this Holy Spirit which binds the group together also works in the life of the individual bringing him to God, but at the same time sending him into the group because it is essentially a spirit of unity.

This doctrine, then, is a theory of community which relates the group to nature, to history, and to the individual personality. This is also the clue to emancipation of the person from mechanization and from enslavement to the group. It is security for the integrity of the human personality ; and it points also toward freedom, which we shall discuss later.

Finally, security requires some core of *meaning* and value. For man cannot live except for values, and his sanity demands that he have some sense of the achievement of value. To be without meaning is to be insecure in the world, for then a man does not know where he stands, what he is, or where his destiny lies. There is no centre of balance in one's life without a fulcrum of meaning ; and there are no criteria of judgment and interpretation by which he can find his place in the world. This is a basic insecurity. At the present time our social order suffers acutely from this sort of insecurity too. Society does not know where it should go, because it does not see clearly the place of human society in the universe, and because it has no adequate basis for appraising its own actions.

Security, then, must be realistic, it must be growing, it must be communal, and it must be meaningful.

II.   UNITY

WE come, then, to the second challenge of the opening chapter : how can we have unity without being enslaved to absolutism ? Dr. Tillich declares that the world already has a physical unity but that its spiritual unity has not been realized. He points out that bourgeois society has been mistaken in thinking that there is an automatic harmony of interests which will assert itself when individual interests are given free play without control, as in the *laissez-faire* theory. Where rational control of social life abdicates, the will to power asserts itself. Free enterprise begets the trust which threatens the small business man. Independent national sovereignty leads to power politics and the dominance of small nations by great. The result is not community but chaos ; for the ends of life are lost sight of in a race for naked power. What is community ? he asks. Is it to be achieved by reason, if that reason has itself become individualistic and self-sufficient ? Can the will to power produce unity ? Or is unity to be found in some higher spiritual purpose that reaches out toward a reality beyond humanity ?

The Christian asserts that adequate community cannot consist of a common bond of blood or soil, for that reduces human life to subhuman terms and denies the reality of culture itself as a medium of unity. It must be more than a community established through communication, for we know that the deepest experiences of the individual are often incommunicable. Purely rational community has a certain artificiality about it which negates the value of private experience. What is required is a form of community which allows indi-

viduality of experience to assert itself while stressing
the bonds of unity in which the person finds his
fulfilment.

But this is precisely the Christian doctrine of brotherhood. This doctrine is not a mere recognition of
common blood or class. It is a declaration of unity
enriched by the very diversity that seems to threaten
unity. For the world is one in which God is moving
through differences into creative novelty, through the
many into single events in which the old meanings of
the many are given new direction and new power.
The new life of the early Church sought this kind of
brotherhood. The *koinonia*, the fellowship, was based
on the universality which allowed differences to be
eagerly embraced rather than sedulously avoided.

There were inevitable struggles in that primitive
community growing out of tensions between people of
different backgrounds and outlooks. They were therefore called to the discipline of love : the discipline
imposed by the determination to find in one another
the personal value that spelled individuality. Mutual
appreciation is too weak a term to use for this ; for
the love that Jesus demanded and exemplified was a
determined effort to find not only what was worthy
of admiration in the other, but also what need of the
other person one could meet from one's own resources.
Consequently mutual confession was more important
than self-assertion ; and humility took precedence over
pride. Such confessed need was a basis for devoted
help from the others, and in this sacrificial devotion
men grew in spiritual stature themselves by realizing
their powers through service. This fundamental condition of creative fellowship was the feature of early
Christianity that Nietzsche missed in his attack, and
his ethics of self-assertion cut off the roots of human
growth despite its noisy declarations about man's
creativity.

We overlook, except in emergencies, the curious paradox that self-sacrifice is the basis of self-realization in the brotherhood. War takes on the aspect of great moral exhilaration because men then realize again that through sacrificial devotion they reach out to new levels of spiritual attainment. The solidarity that ensues is a testimony to this basic truth.

The political theory of democracy is rooted in this view, for it holds that a nation grows by sharing its differences, and that all possible means must therefore be used to assure the maximum exchange of differing opinions (freedom of speech and press), with security from reprisals through secrecy in voting (the secret ballot), after which the elected representatives are under obligation to represent the varying interests of their constituencies in debate over proposed laws (parliament or congress). Thus by " negotiation, compromise and consent," agreement is reached among divergent interests.

The way in which democratic attitudes rest back on Christian principles can be more clearly appreciated if we note the negative factors that imperil democratic processes : selfishness, pride that will not yield in negotiation and makes a farce of it, lack of imagination to perceive the meaning of a situation from within the life of another person or group, confusion regarding the abilities and motives of another. All of these contradict the Christian conception of love as (a) imaginative entrance into the life of another so as to see the situation as from his point of view, (b) determination to feed one's life into his so as to help him to fullest self-realization in that situation, and (c) some criterion of the values of human life in the light of which he may be helped to realize his *highest* possibilities. All three steps are required in Christian love ; for sympathetic imagination may be nothing more than mawkish sentimentalism, while help without identifying one's

life with another may become domineering benefaction,
and either of them, without an adequate view of the
meaning of the world and man's place in it, is open
to tragic error in which he who would save actually
damns another.

But Christianity is not merely a theory of democracy.
It goes further than that, for it is a theory and practice
for all of life, and is therefore more inclusive than
democracy.　While in democratic political theory
individual differences are appraised as contributions to
the life of the group, Christianity sees the individual
as having value in his own right intrinsically, because
he is related to the purpose of God in the world and
finds in that purpose a level of self-realization that
transcends society.　But since God is Himself love, He
conserves in His purpose the freedom and individuality
of man so that human destiny envisages the conservation
of personal identity.　This is the meaning of the
doctrine of immortality, whatever detailed interpretations we may give to that doctrine.　Consequently,
Christianity stands in judgment on every political
theory, and is fully comprehended in none.

In a word, then, Christianity demands that the
interests of other nations, other economic groups,
other races, other families, shall be entered into with
sympathetic appreciation so that we may realistically
understand them.　Then we must know what group
life is meant to be, if we are really to help other groups
to become what under God they should be.　Only
when we have a sense of direction can we be helpful.

The ultimate community is something far profounder
in reality than any of our ideals.　The " Kingdom of
God " is a name for it, and that name reminds us that
it is rooted in God and subject to Him.　This is its
radical character.　In the realm of international
relations it means that a common spiritual aim is
deeper than the economic interdependence which at

N

present dominates our thinking. Some common interest in the fate of humanity as a whole must transform the doctrine of national self-interest. Some common culture embracing the fundamental values and assumptions of human existence is required to give a spiritual footing for schemes of world organization.

The Christian believes that one of these assumptions is found in the Christian principle of *universalism*. All men are related to God, and differences in their historical position as members of different races, classes or educational groupings do not abrogate this relationship. Because of this each man or woman stands in a unique relation to God, and is able to make some individual contribution to the world's life. To make this contribution is both his responsibility and his privilege. Any system, therefore, that denies his individual significance and prevents his making his contribution must, for the Christian, stand under condemnation. For the same reason all forms of discrimination on the basis of race or class, or any other distinctive status in society, which operate to prevent the individual or group from realizing its proper function in the common life and its own full individuality, stand condemned. Concretely this means that in America we must remove the barriers to Negro self-development, to the moral growth of slum-dwellers, to the advancement of the worker, to the usefulness of the aged.

In this sense universalism brings as its corollary the fulfilment of personality. Individualism has always been a concomitant of universalism since the days of Jeremiah and Ezekiel, the one stressing the access of each man to God and the latter the personal responsibility of every man to God. Because every single person has this individual quality, he can make a unique contribution to the enrichment of human corporate life.

There is another implication of the principle of universalism. It abrogates all irresponsible national sovereignty. According to this view, no nation is answerable only to itself. It has a place in the sun and must discharge the responsibilities dictated by its situation. The test of its claims and its duties, and its fulfilment of its life, are through serving the life of the world. But there is no one pattern for the international contribution of the several nations, for each has its own peculiar place. This is the truth in the idea of national destiny, but it has been exaggerated into the doctrine of special saviourhood and has then been hypocritically transformed into a theory of a moral superiority. Then we rationalize the lust for power lying at the root of imperialism, or the egotism called national pride. When the accident of birth is used to furnish a basis for elaborate theories of racial superiority, the human element of responsibility has been forsaken for the lower stage of mere biological peculiarity. Vitalism has then taken the place of spiritual power. The difference between the two is one of the most needed distinctions today, for spiritual power is always in terms of the relation to God while vitalistic energy has no ethical connotations and lands in moral nihilism. When a nation is thus conceived in amoral terms the possibility of international order is nullified so far as that nation is concerned.

Power politics rest on such an amoral view of the nation. Nations are often driven to such an attitude by the denial to them of any reasonable chance for creative life. This must be borne in mind in our thinking about postwar Germany. If a nation cannot develop within the law it will assert itself apart from law and thus precipitate chaos.

This raises the whole problem of the relation of creativity to law, and here we come to another great principle of Christian social philosophy. According to this principle the source of creative activity in the world is the divine purpose. But the creative process has both destructive and constructive aspects. Every instance of creative action involves the destruction of the old pattern of activity. But the destructive phases may gain the upper hand and the creative meaning may itself be destroyed. Every creative moment requires novelty, for apart from newness we cannot recognize anything creative about the activity. Yet the only way in which the new can be identified is by comparison with the old, so that some novel emergent quality is apparent. This new quality cannot be identified, however, unless there is some form, some structure, in the new situation whereby it may be compared with the old structure. Creativity therefore involves both the energy that breaks through the established order and some form or structure of its own. In this way the creative purpose of God is always demanding the destruction of some old order and directing the process toward some new structure. There is both law and overcoming of established law in His activity. This will help us to understand the relation of a Christian philosophy to government and revolution.

Every government is the organization of social values in a definite structure ; and the overthrow of government is always beset by the peril of chaos. However, the growth of social life requires that established forms be transformed and transcended. Where the forms at present in the ascendancy thwart the development of the life of men, the purpose of God requires that they be destroyed. This is the basis of the Christian right of revolution. But as we said above, every revolution releases forces that may be chaotic rather than creative. Some new meaning of positive value must emerge if the creative purpose of God is to be manifest. Hence the need for some criterion of value to justify revolution and to direct peaceful change.

For the Christian this principle is love, and its
corollary is the fulfilment of personality. These define
the equal rights that all men are meant to enjoy. But
the notion of right is here transcended, for the claim
of a " right " is unnecessary where others eagerly reach
out in love to help. Justice is vitalized by love, since
the interests that are reconciled and the rights that are
balanced in justice, are more clearly seen and understood as from within the life of the individual through
the effort of love. One man enters into the life of
another to see it from his standpoint. When this
effort is guided by the realization that every person is
in process of growing, it becomes more apparent that
new interests of his have to be provided for in a just
law.

This is one measure of the tragedy of our American
racial situation. Attitudes developed, and law enacted,
at one stage in the development of the Negro are continued beyond their usefulness. The law becomes
unjust, because the definition of justice sought is now
anachronistic ; its creative character is lost, and law-
abidingness becomes a travesty on justice. Justice is
not opposed to love. It needs love to keep it dynamic
in a changing world. Here is the Christian foundation
of justice in the international scene. Without it any
world organization must fall a prey to legalism ; and
any scheme of domestic social planning will become
another fixation requiring a revolution to break it.

The Church—and Christianity is the only religion
that has a Church—as a body of believers, transcends
nation and race and class in a brotherhood of obligation
to God. But even the Church is not an end but a
means. If it becomes an absolute, it denies the working
within it of the Holy Spirit, the Spirit of God which
is continually re-creating it.

Here lies the meaning of Christian missions. The
Church reaches out beyond its own cultural milieu,

and enters into the life of other cultures, not to sub-ordinate them to Christendom, but to venture out into new historical contexts. In the process it is itself changed in the discharge of its function. Eventually Christendom itself must be transformed, because it is required to be humble before God and to grow through its own missionary effort into something larger, some-thing still more universal, and therefore more representative of God. This has become more apparent as the so-called "Younger Churches" (i.e. the Churches beyond the Western Christian move-ment) have made their valuable contributions at great ecumenical conferences like that of Madras (in 1938) to the enrichment of the Christian message. This is a sample of what might happen among the nations, making a federation of the nations of the world a finer community.

III.　FREEDOM

THE third great word of the opening chapter is freedom. It is set over against the Leviathan of corporate tyranny, whether this be the state or the mechanistic economy of capitalism. In a day when the Four Freedoms are so widely hailed, the basis of true freedom needs to be understood. When France fell in 1940, its keenest citizens saw in this collapse the evil fruitage of a freedom that was irresponsible. It is this freedom that threatens all security and all community ; ending in suicide of freedom itself. Can we have freedom without irresponsi-bility, liberty without licence ?

To this question Christianity replies with a doctrine of freedom that is rooted in responsibility and that enriches community. Each man stands in his own special relation to God who is the source of his being. This defines his uniqueness. At the same time it defines his freedom, for no power on earth except

man's own will can destroy that relation. But the
very awareness of this freedom is a temptation to
assert his independence even of God, the source of his
life ; and this is the radical sin which destroys the
very basis of his freedom. Consequently it is only as
man responds to God that his freedom is guaranteed ;
it is a responsible freedom. Now, God stands in this
same relation to every man ; and therefore one's
responsibility to God becomes also a responsibility for
all men. Freedom is inextricably bound with community.

The social implications of this doctrine of freedom
are far-reaching. In the first place it means that the
personal character of every man must be respected.
This is recognized in the idea of freedom of worship ;
but not so definitely acknowledged in economic life.
The worker tends to be mechanized as a productive
unit performing some operation for which a machine
has not yet been invented. When the machine has
been devised and installed the man can go. Yet today
employers are becoming aware of the influence of the
worker's total personal situation — his worries, his
emotional imbalance, his fatigue — upon his productive capacity ; and so they employ personnel managers.
But the orientation is still false so long as the person
is regarded from the standpoint merely of his productive
power. The moral obligation to the worker *as a person*
is not really discharged.

The problem of the person is more acutely encountered in race relations. When the Negro or the Asiatic
is treated simply as an instance of a racial type, he is
merely representative, not unique as an individual.
His personal identity is lost in his racial status and his
freedom is restricted by the generalization about his
race. His personality is submerged and he is not
respected as a person. Conversely, the member of a
so-called " superior " race may also lose his individuality

in the presence of an exploited people, and be unable to break through to assert his own personal attitude where it stands in contrast with that of his own group. Freedom is lost on both sides of the race conflict.

Christian freedom requires further that a man's unique contribution, born of his unique situation and experience, should be made to the common life. Here we have the real meaning of freedom to work. It is often confused with a capitalistic doctrine of " freedom to work " which seeks to break the community of the workers so that the detached individual may be more easily exploited. But at the same time a union may also prevent a man from doing his best by imposing on him a standard of mediocrity so as to preserve the jobs of men less capable. The criterion lies in enabling the person to give to society all that he has to give, so that maximum personal development may go hand in hand with his best potential contribution to the common good. Differences are here maintained because they stimulate the life of the group. " Diversity of gifts but one spirit " is the Christian formula ; and that one spirit is a loving concern for the well-being of others— a love like the love of God.

To maintain this diversity is a great test of patience, especially where there is pride. It is hard to recognize the virtue of that which is radically different from ourselves. But this is precisely the discipline required of the Christian. Indeed, the Christian must go further and seek fellowship with those who differ, because the fellowship of diverse persons constitutes the creative community which is the hope of the future. *Laissez faire* is here transcended in community of labour and thought ; and planning is given a new meaning because tyranny is avoided. For tyranny is destruction of difference by conformity. In the Christian way men are saved from the two extremes of modern life.

When we apply this same principle to intercultural

relations, whether in the world at large or in the polyglot American population, the result will be a radical change in our accepted practice.   To Americanize is not to impose an Anglo-Saxon pattern on the immigrant, but to allow him freedom to develop his native and cultural gifts so as to create a richer culture among us.   This has actually happened with our music and literature, and even with our religion ; and we may be able to point the way for mankind if we do not lose this vision in the dead uniformity of " the melting pot." What a drastic revolution is demanded in international relations by this principle !   The white man's burden still remains, but the coloured races must help him to bear it because it is theirs too.

Freedom is thus the very basis of responsibility. Recognition of this fact constitutes the strength of progressive education ; but this new movement has often lost its bearing by stressing a type of individualism which does not promote a clearer sense of community with the group.   For personal gifts are meant to be developed as contributions to others' lives.   Mere jealous preservation of diversity is not enough.   The social function of the diversity must be realized through responsible living.   Individual responsibility, in turn, becomes the basis of genuine freedom for others.   This cannot be developed in education except as it is bound into the life of some community.   Such a community-centred educative process may be secured by a reorientation of our whole educational method so that the concrete situations of group life—in the town or in the school community—are the centre of instruction.   This has been tried many times, but, with lack of any clear aims for community life beyond the familiar bourgeois respectability, it could not be fully achieved.   Because community can ultimately find its centre only in God, the humanism of most progressive educational theory is philosophically inadequate.   The religious meaning of social life should appear at the centre of every concrete social plan and every individual decision.

However, it is necessary at once to distinguish this from current proposals for " religious education " in the public school programme. These tend either to foster a fatally shallow and negligible formalism of Bible reading without intelligent understanding or discussion, or to revert to an undesirable sectarianism in which children who discuss all other problems together in democratic fashion are expected to segregate into denominational groups when the deepest concerns of life are under study. The artificial separation of religious and secular thinking is thus aggravated, and the life of religious commitment in the workaday world is made more difficult. Education must reach its religious depth by pushing the analysis of immediate problems to their limits where the dependence of men on God is realized and the basis of personal decision in the Christian way can be explored. Education becomes truly Christian at the point where the meaning of a life centred in Jesus Christ becomes both intelligible and operative in personal action. The person's activity is freed when it is related to realities that transcend our social life, when he finds in the deepest meaning of our world the clue to the resolution of his own inner conflicts, and when, being in harmony with God's will, he is not frustrated by nature.

IV.   MEANING

THIS brings us to the last major problem raised in the first chapter : How are men to be given a sense of meaning in life ? The meaninglessness and the consequent aimlessness and futility that make men fall prey to the lust for power in themselves or in others, constitutes one of the darkest phases of contemporary life. How can we gain a new sense of the meaning of personality? How can we overcome the alienation of self from society and nature? How can we move through mere technical reason to a richer intellectual meaning of the world? If the Christian Gospel, the good news of Christian faith, has any claim to serious consideration, it must give a clear answer to this problem.

We need not elaborate here what has already been said in Chapters 2 and 3 about the meanings that emerge from an analysis of Christian faith. Our task is to see what such meaningfulness implies for social existence. We must at once acknowledge that meaningfulness has a practical reference. It is not restricted to a theoretical system as such but is a clue to action in concrete situations. To use Dr. Tillich's phrase, it is " existential " meaning : that sort of meaning which, in a moment of acute decision, delivers one from hopeless confusion, and rescues one from the fatalistic sense of being caught in the web of circumstances. At the same time it is something more than a knowledge of mechanical techniques. Such knowledge merely shows us *how* to do something, while our urgent need is to know *what* it is that we ought to do.

First of all, the individual needs to feel that he himself means something to the world. Nothing is more tragic than to have a person feel that he has no particular significance for anyone, that he is not even a supernumerary who might fit in in a pinch. The aged, the invalid, the immature all face this tragic experience. What can a Christian say to them? He can say, first of all, that every man or woman or child stands in a unique relation to the world and God so that there is no exact duplicate of him anywhere. Were this a mere statement of difference it would not meet his need, however, for his distinctiveness might be simply abnormal or it might be inconsequential.

The Christian goes further and declares that the individual is related to a divine purpose in which each life has a place. When the individual sees his place in that divine purpose, he acquires significance beyond his present status. This significance is also positively related to his present status, for it is here and now that he can and must work out his meaning in the world. The wealth of experience of the aged may be accompanied by inflexible attitudes or inadequate power of consistent and consecutive thought, but others can nevertheless use that experience in their own decisions ; and it can exert a stabilizing influence on their judgments. We are forced to face this problem by the increasing proportion of old people in our population. If their lives are meaningless, the meaninglessness of American life will be accentuated.

Invalids are often led to the brink of insignificance by the pity of friends whose solicitude deprives them of a sense of usefulness. Then the invalid evades his responsibility, and loses his significance. His task is to find in the face of handicaps some positive clue to conduct. When the maimed and the blind return from military service, this task must be undertaken by them and by their friends courageously as well as sympathetically. The Christian doctrine of the personal responsibility of every person under God is the tonic which overcomes self-pity.

Another way in which the individual loses his meaning is through failure to define his status in a rapidly changing world. Infantilism is the fixation of one's meaning at the level of childish life, when in reality one has passed physiologically into maturity and its social obligations. Hypocrisy is the effort of an individual to maintain different attitudes in different groups, appearing now as the tender father and again as the philanderer, or at one time as a conscientious citizen and at another as a man conniving to destroy the bases of community life through corruption of officials. The " split personality " lives in two rôles without being aware that they conflict ; while the confused man is unable to clarify his rôle in a given situation. Christianity proposes a growing definition of one's rôle, because it recognizes both personal growth and social history, and sees the person as a historical being obligated to redefine his duty. To the hypocrite it throws out the challenge to be consistent in devotion to a consistent God, so that character—which is consistency—may control conduct ; and it probes the secret conflicts of the hidden life in an effort to achieve this consistency.

On the other hand it also accentuates conflict by demanding decision. The murky waters of indecision must now be precipitated in commitment ; and the commitment must be in terms of the ultimate meaning of the situation. Consequently every decision becomes a decision for or against God ; and thereby life reaches a new depth. Only as this acute and desperate stage is reached does a man come face to face with God, and only then can his life really acquire full meaning. It is therefore the task of religion to drive men relentlessly to this stage of thinking because their ultimate salvation depends upon it.

In the background of this personal action lies the social scene. If that be meaningless, it is difficult to see how any person can bring his own rôle to bear fruit and carry meaning. Today this meaning of society is not clearly focussed, because we are preoccupied with technical problems and with immediate, opportunist adjustments. Science and public policy are divorced from philosophic truth. The Christian doctrine of the immanence of God challenges such a divorce.

The most striking and peculiarly Christian form of this doctrine is the dogma of the Incarnation that God became active in and through a man in order to express the meaning of His purpose in human terms. And since God is dynamically involved in life, it follows that no immediate action can be separated from Him. The eighteenth-century Deists taught that God had separated Himself from the world after the creation. By this teaching they removed Him from active participation in the human scene, and paved the way for modern atheism. Thereby they also set the stage for modern social irresponsibility. Society began to lose its sense of destiny and of its own meaning. When Positivism denied the significance of thought about the cosmos, society had nowhere to turn beyond itself for its criteria of judgment. Then it was caught within its own mechanism. The transcendent reference necessary to any prophetic criticism was lacking. Social reform became a reshuffling of social process without any test of its creative significance.

In the Incarnation, however, men have the principle of human life transforming itself through its unity with a divine purpose running through the world. Life is lifted up to a new level of meaning, and social order is subjected to the revolutionary principle of Jesus' revelation of God. Society thus acquires a new creative meaning in which every act is a sacrament, every reform is a test of faith in the Kingdom of God, and every claim to progress is subjected to scrutiny. The world bore a different meaning after Jesus came. Without this faith the full scope of social action cannot be attained. Its clues are those we have already mentioned : security, unity, and freedom.

This suggests the task of reason : to go beyond technical development of means (which is the important and essential function of science) to criticism and clarification of ends. The Frankenstein of modern life is not the machine as such, but highly developed " mechanism " which has outrun man's ability to control it by any purpose of his own. The power he has generated he cannot now direct, and for lack of aims he becomes the victim of its aimlessness. We cannot solve the problem of the machine age with machines, but only with the spirit that goes beyond the " mechanism " to envisage ends. This same principle applies to the mechanisms of his own organic life. His emotional drives and his habits must be brought under the control of purpose. Reason here encounters a dilemma. Thought is unconsciously influenced by vital urges which also give it its energy, and at the same time it is called upon to control these urges.

The solution lies in a different view of human nature than that offered by either rationalism or vitalism. A more inclusive principle, and one that stands above them both, is demanded. Christian thought concerning man, as the third chapter has indicated, offers this more inclusive principle in its conception of the Spirit of God. This Spirit is a spirit of *truth* because it expresses the ultimate reality. It is also a source of *power* because it is the foundation of all energy in the world, being that by virtue of which the world was created. Consequently the Christian turns to God for the overcoming of the dilemma we have described. This assumes that one can apprehend the grace of God, and that by it the contradictions of our own nature are resolved. Apart from this experience, which is called regeneration, there is no hope of solving the problem of thought itself.

There are two interpretations of the world between which we must choose. One regards nature as a self-sufficient whole, carrying within itself the criteria of its own validity. The other views nature as subject to a transcendent, yet immanent, God whose purpose is the criterion for judging nature, society and man. He it is who gives meaning to existence.

What are the implications of this Christian position ?

Clearly that through Jesus Christ human thought is brought both to an impasse because a new basis is introduced for judging all questions, and to a new creative level because in the radical reorientation of thought toward Christ as its centre we can once more come to terms with God. The meaning of all life is then transformed by the central principle of love. But we must never forget that the grace of God transcends all our explications. We must not, therefore, expect history to furnish its own answer to the meaning of the human adventure, but must return to the Gospel for that answer.

How the Christian answer is related to the best of secular thought has been indicated in the second chapter, and the general framework and perspective of the Christian Gospel have been expounded in the third. We have in this chapter tried to state the answer of this Gospel to society's need. What that answer is in terms of Jesus' demands on the individual is the subject of the chapter that is to follow.

CHRISTIANITY AND THE CHRISTIAN

John Knox

THE discussion of this book has moved constantly nearer the individual. It began with an analysis of the contemporary world—a diagnosis of its ills, an adumbration of its hopes and possibilities. This was followed by consideration of some of the intellectual difficulties in the way of modern man's acceptance of the Christian answer to this contemporary crisis. The third chapter contained a statement of what this Christian answer is and a discussion of its relevance to the problems of our age. In the fourth chapter some of the social implications of this faith were elaborated. In all of this we have never been far from the place where each of us as an individual stands. But in the present chapter we shall be concerned entirely, and more explicitly, with the individual, and particularly with what is ultimately his most important problem— the problem which every morally responsible person must face, for the most part separately and alone, with every breath he draws : " What has God called me to be and do and how can I fulfil that vocation ? "

I.   OUR MORAL DILEMMA

WHEN Portia in *The Merchant of Venice* remarks to her maid, " If to do were as easy as to know what were good to do, chapels had been churches and poor men's cottages princes' palaces," she states a principle to which we doubtless find ourselves assenting without question. John Drinkwater in much more serious mood expresses the same idea in one of his poems, "A Prayer," which concludes :

> We know the paths wherein our feet should press,
> Across our hearts are written Thy decrees :
> Yet now, O Lord, be merciful to bless
> With more than these.
>
> Grant us the will to fashion as we feel,
> Grant us the strength to labour as we know,
> Grant us the purpose, ribb'd and edg'd with steel,
> To strike the blow.
>
> Knowledge we ask not,—knowledge Thou has lent,
> But, Lord, the will,—there lies our bitter need,
> Give us to build above the deep intent
> The deed, the deed.[1]

True as this is, however, it is not the truism we might at first suppose. Although our moral need undoubtedly consists primarily not in our lack of knowledge but in the weakness of our moral purpose, still all of us more than occasionally find ourselves in situations where it seems that doing would be easy if only we could see clearly what ought to be done. To mention only one example—although perhaps the crucial one—probably no one of us finds it easy to justify our relatively comfortable way of life in view of the enormity of human need about us. And yet who is clear as to what one ought to do ? In a world where all men, without knowing one another or even of one another's existence, are nevertheless tied in together so intimately, so inextricably, and, as things are, so inequitably, that my gain means all too often another's loss ; my comfort is enjoyed at the price of another's misery ; I profit by the agony of some half-starved Chinese labourer on the other side of the world—in such a

---

[1] John Drinkwater, " A Prayer " ; by permission of the Sidgwick & Jackson.

world, do we not often find ourselves uttering the same prayer as Hamlin Garland voices in a poem which he calls " The Cry of the Age " :

> What shall I do to be just ?
> What shall I do for the gain
> Of the world—for its sadness ?
> Teach me, O Seers that I trust !
> Chart me the difficult main
> Leading me out of my sorrow and madness ;
> Preach me out of the purging of pain.
>
> Shall I wrench from my finger the ring
> To cast to the tramp at my door ?
> Shall I tear off each luminous thing
> To drop in the palm of the poor ?
> What shall I do to be just ?
> Teach me, O Ye in the light
> Whom the poor and the rich alike trust :
> My heart is aflame to be right.[1]

And the mood of this poem is just as authentic as that of Drinkwater's. It is with the problem which these two poems set before us that the present chapter is largely concerned.

II.   CAUSES OF CONFUSION

IT is not necessary to speak at length of the social-historical causes of our moral confusion. The first chapter has already covered that ground. The same developments which have contributed to the intellectual difficulties which the contemporary individual meets in his effort satisfactorily to think through the meaning of his life also deepen and complicate his moral problem. Intellectual and moral experience cannot be separated ; and the terrific tensions which mankind is undergoing

---

[1] Used by permission.

in this revolutionary epoch have placed extraordinary strains upon both our thinking and our being, have shaken the foundations of both religious faith and moral purpose.

Indeed, the whole reality of the moral life has been placed in jeopardy. These are not times ideally adapted to exemplifying the lines,

> When Duty whispers, low, Thou must,
> The youth replies, I can.

But the fault does not lie altogether with youth. Duty herself has become doubtful and equivocal.

This decay of principle is in considerable part an aspect of the fate of absolutes in general which has engaged our attention more than once in this book. At a time when many are disposed to say, " Nothing is absolutely true," it is not strange that the same persons, or others, are saying, " Nothing is absolutely right." The causes of this moral relativism or nihilism are largely the same as of the corresponding intellectual relativism or nihilism, and in so far as this is true it does not need to be discussed here. I shall be content with calling the briefest possible attention to two considerations which apply more specifically to our particular problem.

The first of these is the fact that moral sanctions are so largely social in origin. Our moral characters are formed in social communities ; and one is tempted to say that our earliest judgments of right and wrong are merely the reflections of patterns of belief and behaviour which belong to our particular community. I doubt that this inference is true ; I am inclined to believe that even a child is able to distinguish vaguely between the conventional and the right, between what he must do because his parents command it and what he must do because God commands it—just as I believe he distinguishes very early between accidental fact and necessary, *a priori* truth. But there is no denying the intimate involvement of social and ultimate sanctions in our moral judgments. Now it is clear that the authority of these merely social sanctions has been seriously undermined. In the kind of world described in the first chapter of this book men have been uprooted —ideologically and spiritually, if not physically—from the communities in which they and their fathers were reared. They are forced to feel the inadequacy, the irrelevance, the lack of foundation, of many of their inherited moral beliefs and habits. Under these circumstances, whether they realize it or not, they face a crisis in the moral sphere. Unless they can lay firm, fresh hold upon the elements in their moral heritage which rest for their authority not upon the mores of a community but upon the will of God, they face the danger of complete moral disintegration.

The second particular source of danger lies in the considerable mechanization of life in the modern period. The moral life is essentially personal : it belongs intimately to *persons* and is concerned with their relations with other *persons*. Whatever tends to dull or to destroy my awareness of myself as a person in relation with other persons strikes at the very roots of the moral life. No wonder, then, that in a period when our social relationships have been more and more depersonalized, there has been a decay in morals.

But the principal fact making for moral confusion was referred to at the very beginning of this chapter. It is the sheer size and complexity of the field in which the moral life of the modern man is to be exercised. As he looks out upon his world—a world so hopelessly distraught, so desperately in need—he seems to confront an impossible ethical task and is in danger of admitting himself defeated without a battle. To this fact we shall return again.

It is possible to exaggerate the importance of the

distinctive character of a particular historical epoch.
Man's fundamental problems—intellectual and moral
—are perennial problems growing out of permanent
elements in himself and in his world. Moral character
no more than intellectual assurance is easy in any age.
No one will be likely to deny, however, that in our
own period the position of both is more than usually
precarious.

Before discussing at greater length our fundamental
and continuing moral problem, especially as the
Christian sees it and must deal with it, I should like
to append to this section two very simple cautions.

First, we must not permit a recognition of the
complicated character of our moral obligations to
make us less responsible in the carrying through of
the obligations we can more or less clearly see. My
father, who died twenty years ago, was far less aware
of the range of his ethical obligations than I have
been made of mine ; he was not greatly troubled by
any number of matters which to me have serious ethical
implications ; but I am pretty sure that my father
was a more downright honest man than I am, that
it would have hurt him more to tell a lie whether in
his words or deeds, that he did his day's work with
greater fidelity than I do mine, that in the somewhat
more limited area in which his moral life was lived
he acted with greater decision and maintained a deeper
integrity.

The second caution is this : we must not let confusion
as to how we ought to act, in respect to the injustices
and cruelties of our social order, make us callous to
their reality or paralyze any attempt at amelioration.
The bitterest charge the prophet Amos can bring
against the privileged classes among his contemporaries
is that they were not " grieved for the affliction of
Joseph." It is one of the marks of maturity that as
we grow older we become less sanguine than we once

were able to be about the effectiveness of any proposed
remedy for the world's ills. But that maturity has
been purchased at too high a price if we lose our
sensitiveness to the reality of those ills and cease to be
terribly, poignantly concerned about them.

III.   GOD'S PERFECT WILL

OUR moral problem has been described as consisting
both in a lack of assurance of what our duty is and
in a lack of power to do it. We must now undertake
a more careful analysis of this two-fold moral need.
We can appropriately begin with a reference to the
ethical teachings of Jesus, which for the Christian have
a peculiar value and authority.

It will be generally granted that the ethical teachings
of Jesus, while clarifying our situation and pointing
the way to the solution of many of our ethical difficulties,
also serve to confront the Christian with his most fundamental and perplexing ethical problem. This problem
is created by his recognition, on the one hand, of the
absolute truth of Jesus' ethical teachings and, on the
other, of his own inability to keep them. No serious
person who has even begun to see the meaning or
feel the force of Jesus' teachings and life can escape
this predicament. This impracticability of an ethical
ideal, in whose ultimate truth we cannot avoid feeling
the fullest confidence, constitutes the essential problem
of Christian ethics.

This authority of the ethical teachings of Jesus does
not consist in the fact that they are *his* teachings, but
in their own intrinsic truth, to which our own consciences bear witness. I am referring here, not to
Jesus' " easier " sayings, but to those most characteristic
teachings of his, in which we are commanded to deny
ourselves and to commit ourselves unreservedly, passionately, joyously to seeking the good of others ; to his

requirement of love—not mere disinterestedness, but active, self-sacrificial good will ; to his demand for complete sincerity, simplicity, purity, and truth.   In other words, I am referring to those teachings of Jesus which cause us the greatest trouble, whether we are ordinary readers of the Gospels or make some claim to being expert interpreters.   At first sight the source of this trouble seems to be simply that the teachings are impracticable ; at this stage we may either dismiss Jesus as a hopeless visionary or else persuade ourselves that he did not mean what he seems to have said. But we soon find that we cannot so easily get rid of these hard sayings.   We realize that they trouble us not simply because they are impracticable but because they are also true.   We recognize that if Jesus had not defined the will of God in such absolute, uncompromising terms, he *should* have done so.   No lesser terms would have sufficed at all.   Although we would not have seen our duty if Jesus had not pointed it out to us, now that he *has* pointed it out, we have no doubt that it *is* our duty.   We know this not simply because he has commanded it, but because we recognize it to be the will of God and the law of our own being.   We feel ourselves to be under the law of love, which knows no limits and makes no concessions whatever to our selfishness and pride.

This law, we see equally clearly and surely, we do not and cannot perfectly keep.   To be sure, I have occasionally heard someone affirm virtual perfection of some other person, but only in the case of an obvious crank now and then have I heard anyone affirm it of one's self.   But if the demands of God involve our inner as well as our outer lives, our thoughts and motives as well as our deeds and words (and every one of us recognizes that this is true), it is clear that no one is in position to know the relevant facts about a man's relation to the will of God so well as the man himself. Even he is certain not to know all the relevant facts. Still, if he is reasonably honest and intelligent, he will know enough to be sure that he is leaving undone much that he ought to do and that he is doing much that he ought not to do and that by thought, word and deed he is constantly violating the perfect will of God. (Those who say that we have never tried the ethic of Jesus and cannot call it impracticable until we do try it are quibbling. Surely no better proof of the impracticability or impossibility of Jesus' ethic under historical conditions would be needed than the fact that it had never been tried. But I would deny the premise—that it has never been tried. The problem we are discussing would not arise except for persons who have in some real sense tried to obey the law of Christ.)

This inability to obey God's perfect will must thus be charged for the most part to our moral weakness, rather than to any uncertainty about what God's will is. Our basic moral need consists in the lack of power to be and do what we see clearly enough we ought to be and do. We lack the will to be even as righteous as we see our way to being. " Here lies our bitter need." The apostle Paul, who, although many of his terms seem alien and meaningless to the modern reader, came nearer to understanding our moral situation than any of the " moralists ", voices this bitter need in a great passage in his letter to the church at Rome : " The good that I would I do not : but the evil which I would not, that I do. . . . I find then a law, that, when I would do good, evil is present with me. For I delight in the law of God after the inward man : but I see another law in my members, warring against the law of my mind, and bringing me into captivity to the law of sin which is in my members. O wretched man that I am ! who shall deliver me from the body of this death ? " (Rom. 7 : 19–24). Is there any one of us who has not at some time uttered a cry like that, although there was probably no one to hear it except God ?

Indeed, it is this moral impotence which is the major cause of our moral confusion. If we were able to do all that we see we ought to do, we would be able to see more clearly our whole duty. If we could overcome our private selfishness entirely, we would be able to see the needs of others and our own obligations to others in truer perspective. In a word, our problem of not knowing what we ought to do—or the greater part of that problem, at least—can ultimately be traced back to our moral failure, our failure to do what we know we ought to do. Drinkwater is right : God *has* written His decrees across our hearts, and our principal trouble in the last analysis does not lie in ignorance of what those decrees are. It arises rather from the fact that we find perfect obedience to them beyond our power, whether of doing or willing. We cannot keep God's perfect law, and God is not willing to give us an imperfect one. We therefore try to devise one for ourselves ; and in that attempt lies one major source of our confusion. We do not know what we ought to do because we have already decided not to do what we know we ought.

It is significant that whereas Drinkwater's lines are addressed to God, Garland's question is addressed to the wise men : there is no need to ask God that question for all its genuineness and poignancy. With a ring on my finger which would support a man and his family for a year, I confront the poor man " at my door." I know what my duty ultimately is ; my problem arises out of my unwillingness—or my inability, if you like—to do that duty. God says : " Sell whatsoever thou has, and give to the poor, and thou shalt have treasure in heaven (Mk. 10 : 21). . . . Give to him that asketh thee, and from him that would borrow

of thee turn not thou away " (Mt. 5 : 42). God says
this not merely in the Gospel but directly to me as I
stand there facing the needy man. But I answer :
" God, I cannot do that ; thou seest that I cannot do
that ; and since I cannot, wilt thou not tell me what
to do *short* of that ? " But God does not again reply.
He has nothing more to say. God does not dilute his
righteousness. He does not pare down His demands
to suit my desires. We are constantly trying to induce
God to lower His standards so that He can give moral
approval to our conduct, and we often convince ourselves that He has done so. But some sharp reminder
of how far we have fallen short of even our own
standards, much less of God's, shatters our complacency
and we cry, " O God, have mercy upon me, a sinner."

In a word, our moral failure follows principally from
our lack of purpose and power. We know, or con-
ceivably might know, the perfect will of God, but we
lack the will to do it. Sacrifices are called for, which
we are unwilling to make and unable to make ourselves
willing to make, and which, I believe one can reverently
add, even the grace of God is unable to make us
willing to make. God's grace can bring us to repentance
and, in response to faith, can wonderfully renew our
will to righteousness ; but perfect goodness in historical
man is beyond even God's power to create. Only
when His Kingdom shall have come shall His will be
done perfectly on earth. One does not have to be a
student of history, one has only to watch one's self a
little while, to know that this is true.

IV. SIN AND FINITUDE

THE person who thus watches himself will realize that
one element in his moral failure is sin, although he
may not call what he finds by that name. He will
recognize that his failure to do the perfect will of God

—which he knows to be the perfect law of his own life—does not follow simply from limitations upon his power for doing good, but also from the presence in him of positive evil. He finds in himself a positive disposition to sensuality, pride and love of power at which his better nature—his true nature—revolts but from which he is unable to free himself, however much he strives. Indeed, sometimes it seems to him that his slavery to sensuality or pride is only confirmed by his struggles to overcome it. This is true because it is man's capacity for self-consciousness which makes sensuality and pride possible (animals are neither proud nor sensual), and our efforts to overcome them are likely to accentuate our consciousness of self and tighten this hold of our sins on us.

This perverse selfishness, of which man is the victim, manifests itself in cruder and in more subtle ways. It is never far from us—even in our most exalted moments. In the very midst of some generous act we are likely to see it cynically watching us or hear its mocking laugh. It spoils and corrupts even our best ethical achievements ; and the most saintly have been most keenly aware of its presence.

It is a mistake, however, to suppose that our moral problem consists simply in our sinfulness. Although the examples he chose were perhaps not the most appropriate, there is truth in Hamlin Garland's poem. It is perhaps too much to say that " What shall I do to be just ? My heart is aflame to be right " is " the Cry of the Age ", at least in the sense of being at all conscious or articulate, but it is the cry of many millions in our age in many of the situations in which they must make moral choices. Though our individual selfishness and pride are the major cause of our moral perplexity, they are not the sole cause of it. I should like to mention three other causes, although they cannot always be nicely distinguished from one another.

I. We are inevitably limited by the past. We have to live and work within a society which has actually taken form and on which the moral failure of other generations as well as of our own has left its mark. No individual could escape entirely from participation in the injustices and cruelties of the world without ceasing to exist altogether. No white man in present-day American society, for example, can either fully share in the disabilities of the Negro, no matter how much he may wish to do so, or cease to profit by the exploitation of the Negro, no matter how hateful to him that exploitation may be.

This is a dangerous point to make. We could all go much further than we do in dissociating ourselves from the sinful acts of society. Our own personal selfishness is *always* involved along with the inequitable organization of society. And it is always dangerously easy to disclaim *any* responsibility when one is justified in disclaiming entire responsibility. Still, the individual has not begun to see adequately his moral situation if he does not recognize that he is participating in sinful operations of ghastly proportions from which it is not in his power to escape.

II. Related to this inescapable involvement in an imperfect and corrupt social order are certain apparently ineluctable limitations of human nature which the necessity of living in that kind of order makes manifest and to which it imparts something of its own taint. In view of the desperate needs of humanity it would appear that nothing short of complete commitment of life to its service is required. The whole of life must be brought into obedience to love ; that is, to moral good will. This means that all of life must have moral quality ; there is no room left for the *unmoral* or *amoral* in a world so critically needy. One must serve either God or self ; one must be either for or against one's brethren. In a more fortunately situated world there might be room for some middle position ; in ours there is not. To let men die is to kill them ; to be morally indifferent is to be immoral. The world's plight seems to demand the complete consecration of life to social service. Yet, man is apparently not made to stand the strain of such consecration. We are apparently by nature self-centred, although capable of responding sympathetically to another's need. In any kind of approximately ideal society, the needs of others would not be so many or of such kind as to place an impossible demand upon man's capacity for response. But in our society this is not true. The needs of others are so desperately great that a natural self-centredness passes inevitably into a sinful selfishness.

This same desperateness of need in society also has the effect of placing a certain unnatural moral strain upon our family life and upon our life together in other intimate, " natural " groups. In any ideal social order, it is clear that such life is altogether appropriate and innocent. It belongs to man's original nature and as such carries no taint of sin. Although it involves a measure of self-centredness on the part of the several participants in the group, it is self-centredness actually expressing itself in self-giving to other members of the group and is quite compatible with all the sharing of life with persons outside of the group which the situation calls for. But what happens when such intimate-group life is set in the midst of a desperately needy world ? At once a quite unnatural moral strain is placed upon it. One's love for the members of one's family comes into a kind of conflict with one's obligations to the more needy members of the families of others. And the morally sensitive person is made to recognize that his very loyalty to his family and friends involves him in some measure of failure in his obligation to the larger community. Again, a natural affection seems to pass by imperceptible steps into a sinful narrowness.

Not only is man by nature self-centred, he is also by his true nature creative (or, perhaps more truly, designed to be the channel of God's creative power). But creativity requires leisure, relaxation, freedom from tension. One creates for the joy of creation—whether one be a poet, an artisan, a scientist, a scholar, a husband or father, a friend—and not because one is under a moral compulsion to do so for the common good. The complete moralization of life would mean the considerable sterilization of life. But again, how can we escape the obligation of bringing all of life under the constraint of the moral ideal in view of the tragic need of humanity about us? What moral justification can one find for working for the simple joy of working when one might be ministering to the desperate needs of one's fellows? And yet to cease from such free activity would be to cease being human in one of the noblest meanings of that term. Thus, again, a necessary creative freedom passes, it would seem inevitably, into a sinful irresponsibility.

We are forced to conclude that in a sinful and desperately needy world we are incapable, *simply in virtue of our being human*, of perfect obedience to the demands of love, whatever might be true in a world less corrupt and distraught. We cannot define our obligation short of bearing the sins of the world, but it is not within our power even to bear our own. Only God can carry so intolerable a load. That He does so is the meaning of the Cross.

III. Finally, one must recognize that there is often a moral ambiguity in the objective social situation itself in which we must act. Here is where Hamlin Garland's lines particularly apply. This moral ambiguity exists for three principal reasons.

First, in many situations where a moral choice has to be made, one has to decide not between one's own personal interests and those of another, but between the interests of *two* others. This is somewhat true when one must choose between serving one's own family or the more needy families of others. In this case, individual self-interest is involved, because of the intimate way in which one is identified with one's family ; but surely it would be wrong to ascribe simply to selfishness or pride a man's decision to place the needs of his own family before the same needs (or even the slightly greater needs) of others. In such a case he is not choosing simply between himself and another. The major interests involved are *all* those of others.

The same principle is involved when one is called on to take part in a conflict in which one's own interests are not involved but in which what one feels to be the just rights of another are in jeopardy. In such a situation one may find one's self apparently denying love by striking against an aggressor. But this apparent denial of love may grow not out of selfishness or pride but out of what seem to be the demands of love itself. Sometimes one cannot defend the weak without attacking the strong. In other words, there seem to be situations in which love must either be regarded as irrelevant or else must apparently deny itself. In such situations our perplexity does not grow simply out of our unwillingness or inability to do all that love requires (although this may always be involved in some measure) but out of a certain ambiguity in the situation itself. To express love at all in some situations one must seem to deny it. Jesus said : " If any man smite you on one cheek turn the other also " ; here the situation is relatively simple—you and your enemy. But Jesus did not say : " If any man smite one of your friends, lead him to another friend that he may smite *him* also."

Not only is it clear that Jesus could have made no such statement, but also that he would have felt that the involvement of the interests of others (that is, others besides one's self and one's enemy) transformed the whole moral situation and placed our obligations with respect to it in a radically different light.

Another source of ambiguity lies in the fact that each one of us is not simply an individual but functions inevitably in certain representative capacities. A man or woman, for example, is likely to be the head or one of the heads of a family. If the family as a whole is willing to make certain sacrifices of its own interests for the common good, the ethical position is relatively clear. But does the individual, even if he sees clearly that the sacrifices should be made, have the right to make them if they are to rest also—perhaps, even more heavily—upon other persons who do not see their duty as he sees it ? This problem must constantly confront the Christian statesman. In some measure it confronts every Christian citizen.

The third source of ambiguity lies in the apparent impossibility of maintaining social order (or of radically revising it) without resort to the use of non-moral or immoral means. The methods of which love can most congenially and, it would appear, most appropriately make use are methods which always deal with persons as persons in the full sense and therefore treat them as free and sovereign. Love seeks to bring about changes in men's behaviour by bringing about changes in their hearts and minds. It prefers to work from within, not from without ; to work *with* others, not upon them. Its characteristic methods are those of rational appeal and moral suasion, expressed in words and deeds. It prefers to suffer rather than to inflict suffering. The Christian, as we have seen, recognizes the law of love as having ultimate authority and he is sure that only by its characteristic methods can good

P

be created. Indeed, love is, almost by definition, the creative principle in social life.

But apparently the creation of good is not the only ethical task which needs to be done : evil must be restrained. And for this restraint of evil, methods are apparently necessary which love finds uncongenial, if not impossible. The Christian man is certain that the creation of good itself involves, as a by-product, the restraint of evil ; but he also recognizes that at times, because of sin, this restraining work must be undertaken separately and directly, and by coercive means which love dislikes to use. The first Christians, because they expected the early end of history and were able to think of themselves as aloof from political responsibility, simply acknowledged the necessity of force and left the exercise of it to others. The modern Christian, who does not expect the early end of history and who therefore feels under political responsibility, cannot thus absolve himself. In this way he finds himself forced to undertake the restraint of evil with means which endanger the growth of good. Love itself seems to force him to make use of methods of which love cannot easily make use. Here also is involved not necessarily or simply an individual moral failure, but an ambiguity in the situation in which one is called upon to act : it seems that in that situation one cannot follow love without also denying it.

To sum up this long section of the discussion : Our moral failure can be traced principally to what has traditionally been called sin, a certain disposition toward sensuality and pride and love of power, which even the best person is unable successfully to resist. But to stop there would be to oversimplify man's moral situation. First, we must live in a society on whose institutions and customs the sin of other generations and of men generally has left its mark, and in whose unjust and inhuman operations every one of us is involved. Second, the world's suffering puts a strain upon our capacity for conscious moral response to the needs of others which it is not within our human nature to bear. An attempt at the full discharge of our duty would seem to involve at first a thwarting of many of our free, creative impulses, and eventually, if carried far enough, illness, insanity, or death. Finally, the situation in which we are called upon to express love is often morally ambiguous—that is, one is forced to take sides in conflicts where the winning or conserving of values seems to involve also the sacrifice of other values, and where the cry, " What shall I do to be just ? " has a peculiar relevance and poignancy.

The New Testament writers were sure that man is hopelessly in the grip of demonic powers of evil. We probably do not find such a statement either credible or altogether intelligible. That dissent is of minor importance provided we recognize that the biblical terms answer to a profound and permanent fact in human experience : we are the slaves of sin—that is, we are prevented by forces beyond our power to control from fulfilling the righteousness which we know to be the law of our own being—and we are incapable of extricating ourselves from our plight. The recognition of that fact is the first step toward salvation. Only one who cries, " God have mercy upon me, a sinner," is in position to see the deliverance which " the God and Father of our Lord Jesus Christ " offers to all who will receive it.

V.   THE GRACE OF GOD

So far we have been discussing the will of God and our failure to keep it. That will is disclosed in Christ to be the unlimited and unqualified love of others, and our consciences confirm that understanding of God's demand. But this disclosure of the will of God is inseparable from the revelation of the moral *nature* of God.   God requires love because He *is* love.   In the nature of the case this must be true.   Could we conceive of God as requiring that we forgive seventy times seven times if He were not ready to forgive to the uttermost ?   or as asking us to love our enemies if He did not send His rain upon the good and the evil ; or as demanding that we take up our cross if He were not bearing His ?   An immoral God might require many of the external observances in which religion has often seemed to exhaust itself, but only a just God could require justice and only a loving God could require love.   I do not mean simply that it would not be right, or consistent, for an unloving God to require love, but that the requirement itself would be impossible. If it is true, then, that in our heart of hearts we know that God *requires* love, we know also that He *is* love. The revelation of the *will* of God is also a revelation of the *grace* of God.

This truth Jesus' teachings and life amply illustrate. I have said that in him God's will is disclosed ; but that will is not disclosed as a mere law.   God's will for us as Jesus apprehended it could no more be reduced to the terms of law than could a true father's will for his children be written exhaustively into rules.   God's will for us, as we have seen, was love—love toward all, everywhere, always, and without limit.   But as one reads the sayings of Jesus in which this under- standing of God's will is most clearly and movingly expressed, one may well be in doubt whether Jesus' primary intention was to say something about man's duty or about God's nature.   As a matter of fact, the two were inseparably associated in his mind.   It is because God is perfectly good that we can be content with nothing short of perfect goodness.   The meaning of human goodness is determined by the nature of God. We must be loving because God is love.

But this love of God has, quite obviously, two effects :
(1) it lays on us, as we have seen, the complete obligation of love of others, but (2) it also opens the way
to forgiveness for our inevitable failure to discharge so
impossible an obligation.   Here, we have the clue to
the understanding of what appears at first to be an
utter paradox in the Christian position : How can
God's moral demands be real if He stands ready to
forgive to the uttermost ? Does not the grace of God
destroy the reality of the law of God ? Do we not in
effect deny the truth of all we have been saying about
our ethical obligations when we now talk about the
forgiving love of God ? To put into question form
some words of Paul, " How can God be just and the
justifier of the unjust ? " Or, if one wishes to state
the paradox in another way, " How can I know myself
to be unjust if I also know that God justifies me ? "
    The answer lies in the nature of God as love.   It is
from this nature that both the obligation and the
forgiveness flow.   We have not truly understood the
attitude we *should* take toward others if we do not
understand the attitutde God *does* take toward us.
We have not truly understood the will of God if we
do not apprehend also, in that same act of understanding, the forgiveness of God.   And (to answer the
antinomians, who deny the necessity of obedience, as
well as the legalists, who deny our need of grace) we
do not understand the forgiveness of God if we do
not in that same moment know ourselves to be under
the will of God.   I referred just now to Paul as
apparently having struggled with the question : " How
can God be just and the justifier of the unjust ? "
When the question is asked in that way, we cannot
help feeling with Paul a logical difficulty.   But although
the teaching of Paul is at all essential points close to
Jesus' own, nevertheless I feel sure that Jesus could
not have been troubled by any such question.   For

he saw more clearly than Paul that it is in the nature
of love both to require and to give ; to ask everything
and to offer everything.   In Jesus' story of the Prodigal
Son, only the elder brother, who does not know what
it means to love, is disposed to ask, when his father
receives with joy his penitent brother, " How can you
be just and the justifier of the unjust ? "   Everyone
else knows that the father is acting in exactly the
appropriate way ; that he is behaving just as a father
ought to behave ; that his behaviour is not only natural,
but (given the fact of love on his part and penitence
on the part of the son) logical and right.   For love has
a logic and a justice of its own.   There is a justice
which belongs to the family as certainly as there is a
justice which belongs to the law court.   For Jesus the
justice of God was the justice of a Father ; such justice
is not less just for being swallowed up in love.   There
is no limit to God's moral demand upon us simply
because there is no limit to His love for us.

Does not one of the most important differences
between Jesus and Paul lie just here, as our own use
of the familiar phrase of Paul's in the preceding para-
graph suggests ?   For Paul there is apparently a conflict
between the righteousness of God and the grace of
God, which for Jesus, so far as we can gather from
his recorded teachings, did not exist.   Perhaps the
reason for this dichotomy in Paul's thought lies in the
fact that for a long time he knew God as righteous
and then suddenly in his experience of Christ he came
to know Him as love.   If challenged, he would, of
course, have agreed that the God whom he knew in
Jesus Christ as forgiving love was the same God whom
he had always worshipped.   He says as much many
times.   Yet the synthesis for Paul was never altogether
complete.   When Marcion several generations later
erected upon Paul's letters the doctrine of two Gods—
one of justice and the other of love, one of law and the

other of grace—he was not building upon an entirely imaginary foundation.

But Jesus is truer to the central affirmation of Judaism : " The Lord is one God." Jesus lays as much emphasis as Paul does upon the grace of God. Jesus is more aware than Paul is of man's hopeless inability to fulfil the will of God. To be sure, one feels that Jesus was more sensitive to our lack of sufficient devotion to the good, and Paul, to the presence in us of irresistible inclinations toward evil. Jesus is more aware of the good we do not do ; Paul, of the evil we do. But such a difference, if it exists, is one only of degree, and in any case is of minor importance. Both would agree that we are utterly incapable of fulfilling God's perfect will. Jesus lays as much stress as Paul upon our constant need for God's forgiving love. But for Jesus the integration of love and justice within the character of God was more harmonious and complete. He thought of God as Father ; and he knew that fathers can be loving without ceasing to be just and can be just without ceasing to be loving. He knew, indeed, that fathers cannot be just unless they are also loving and cannot be truly loving unless they are also just. Thus, for him, the fact that the God who lays the duty of absolute love upon us is ready to forgive to the furthest limit of our failure created no problem. It was a mystery, but it was the familiar mystery of love. The very demand that we love others is possible only because God loves us. Thus, I repeat, we cannot really feel the force of God's demand unless we in that same moment see the way to forgiveness open before us.

To be sure, penitence is necessary. But penitence is simply realization. It is " coming to one's self." It is becoming aware of one's moral situation. It is the act of apprehending the fact not alone of one's sin but also of God's goodness. For we cannot truly appreciate the nature of our failure unless we recognize God's love. This is true because our sin consists not in a failure to keep the *law* of God but in a denial, a repudiation, of the *love* of God. We have crucified Christ afresh. This is the true, inward nature of our sin, and penitence is the recognition of that true nature. It is thus not an arbitrary condition to that renewal of fellowship with God, which is the meaning of forgiveness, but is a necessary prerequisite, since fellowship can never exist except in sincerity and truth. But clearly repentance is not remorse or despair. If one knows one's self to have violated the *love* of God (and one does not truly *repent* until this is true, no matter how desperately regretful or even remorseful one may be otherwise), one knows also that this same love yearns to forgive and restore one. Thus penitence and faith are not two attitudes, but one. Both consist essentially in a recognition of and response to the love of God, and the one attitude always involves the other. One is a recognition of what I have done to the love of God ; the other of what the love of God yearns to do for me.

What God yearns to do is to restore us to fellowship, to reconcile us to Himself (to use Paul's phrase), to bring us back into the relationship of sons again. I say " back again " because we know intuitively that this relationship represents our true nature and destiny ; that in being alienated from God we are also alienated from our true selves. This consciousness of really belonging to God but of having been separated from Him lies back of the myths of the Creation and the Fall in Genesis, and the authenticity and poignancy of that consciousness makes these ancient stories forever true and relevant. It is that consciousness which gives to Jesus' story of the lost son its universal and timeless appeal. We know *ourselves* to be prodigal sons—really belonging to the Father's house but estranged from

Him. And the essence of the Christian Gospel is simply that God is waiting to receive and restore us : And " when he was yet a great way off, his father saw him, and had compassion, and ran, and fell on his neck, and kissed him. And the son said unto him, Father, I have sinned against heaven and in thy sight, and am no more worthy to be called thy son. But the father said to his servants, Bring forth the best robe and put it on him ; and put a ring on his hand, and shoes on his feet. And bring hither the fatted calf, and kill it . . . for this my son was dead, and is alive again ; he was lost, and is found." (Lu. 15 : 20 ff.).

For being saved, we realize when we " come to ourselves," is not finding one's self, but being found of God. The self-possession we seek is really the actuality of being possessed by Him. Sometimes we talk about freedom as though it were something we desired ; in a very true sense, however, it is the one thing we do not desire, the one thing we cannot bear. The human quest is not, primarily, a search for things we can own, but a search for the one thing to which we can feel justified in belonging. We are always losing our hearts to something—perhaps to a child, or a woman, or a cause. When we lose them, we are at length rich and free ; when they come back to us, as they so often do, we are bound and poor again. What we call our freedom is really our experience of belonging to something completely and irrevocably.

For man does not really possess himself or integrate his own life ; something above him possesses him and integrates his life. And the adequacy of the integration depends upon the adequacy of the possessor. A man's life does not consist in the abundance of the things which he possesses ; it consists in the worth of the one thing that possesses him. Men in their desperate search for life and freedom are constantly trying to give themselves with ultimate devotion to values

which are not worthy or great enough to possess them.
That is idolatry, slavery, disillusionment, death. We
live in any sense that matters, not in the measure we
own ourselves (we never own ourselves), but in the
measure we belong to the only reality which is worthy
or, in the long run, able to possess us, that is, to the
Eternal Truth, Beauty, and Love (whom we often
know without knowing His name) whose service is
perfect freedom. That is what God is—the One to
whom it is our nature to belong, for He has made us
for Himself. No wonder we are restless till we find
rest in Him, are bound until He lays His strong hand
on us, in bondage until we become His slaves, dead
until we give up our lives to Him. That is what Paul
meant when he said, " I live, yet not I, but Christ
lives in me." No man truly lives until he dies that
God may live in him.

VI.   THE NEW LIFE

THE new relationship with God which is wrought by
His grace in response to our repentance and faith is
more than forgiveness, especially if forgiveness is thought
of simply as pardon or what Paul and the theologians
call "justification." To be sure, one knows one's self
to be pardoned, but that pardon is only an aspect of
a larger whole—the restoration to sonship. The father
in Jesus' story can hardly be said to have pardoned
his son when he saw him afar off and had compassion
and ran to meet him : he had pardoned him long
since—if indeed perfect love ever needs to pardon at
all, since it thinketh no evil and suffereth long and is
kind. What the father does is to receive and restore
his son. The elder son—who is not a son at all—
notices that his brother's offences have been pardoned ;
the father has not even thought of it. For him the
significant fact is that he who was dead is alive again ;

he who was lost has been found. Of course, one is forgiven : but the forgiveness is not a legal pardon ; it is reconciliation ; it is knowing one's self to be known and loved of God ; it is restoration to that relationship to God in which we were created to stand.

In that relationship new moral resources are available to us. What we cannot do God does in us. The earlier part of this chapter was devoted to pointing out that moral perfection is beyond the capacity of historical man to attain. Only in the Kingdom of God, which is either beyond history or is a radically transformed history, can such righteousness be possible. This is undoubtedly true ; but it is also true that in the measure we are brought into our true relation with God, resources are released which we ourselves cannot command. Although sin is not destroyed, we become able more successfully to resist it ; and though our human finitude is not transcended, our moral powers are renewed. A power not our own enters and energizes our wills.

For, whether one recognizes and acknowledges it or not, the highest goodness in human life is not of man's construction, but of God's creation. Legalism is an attempt to build goodness by laying one brick upon another. Only a spurious and sterile goodness can be *built*. True and fruitful goodness is alive and organic, and man cannot make it, no matter how desperately hard he tries. Indeed, his tense effort may get in the way of God's creative activity, as such effort often keeps an artist from producing his best work— and for the same reason. True goodness in human life is God's goodness. We must so desire it as to be willing to sacrifice everything for it and then be able simply to wait in utter humility for God to bring it to pass.

This is not to deny the necessity of moral effort.

Only one who has sought—indeed, who constantly seeks—to obey the perfect will of God is capable of the repentance which opens the way to God's creative work. Some of Paul's antagonists seem to have said derisively : " Then why not sin the more that grace may the more abound ? " Many—the so-called anti-nomians—appear to have asked the question seriously. But the question ignores the meaning of repentance. Grace can be effective for forgiveness only in so far as we repent—and the possibility of repentance ceases when the effort to obey the will of God is slackened. That man is under obligation to strive to fulfil the will of God, Paul, no more than Jesus, thought of denying. Both agree that he never escapes from this obligation. The point, which Jesus as well as Paul is constantly making, is that God does not wait till we have dis-charged this obligation to grant us His grace. While we are yet sinners, God loves us and offers not only pardon but fellowship. But this pardon and fellowship cannot be received except by the penitent ; and one cannot repent who does not feel the constraint of the will of God. Thus, although our salvation does not wait upon the perfection of our obedience, it does wait upon the sincerity of our submission. Only to one who is seeking to subject himself in everything to love as demand can God's love disclose itself as grace. The love of God must constrain us if it is also to save us. Only one who, in the light of the revelation of the love of God in Christ, knows the reality of his sin and recognizes his impotence to do God's perfect will is in position to receive the forgiveness and new life which that same love freely offers and longs to bestow.

The person to whom the grace of God is thus vouchsafed will be under no illusion that the roots of selfishness and pride have been destroyed in him. He will be constantly reminded of his need of God's forgiveness. The despairing cry of Paul to which I

have referred, " O wretched man that I am ! Who
will deliver me from this body of death ? ", is not the
cry of a stranger to the mercy of God, but of one to
whom God has made Himself known as love but who
still finds in himself a law which wars against the law
of his mind, continually thwarts his better, truer nature,
and holds constantly over him the threat of slavery
and death. But the power of sin, though not destroyed,
is broken, and a righteousness not his own is miraculously
created within him : " I thank God through Jesus
Christ ! For what the Law could not do, God did by
sending His own son. . . . He sentenced sin to death
that the righteousness of the Law might be fulfilled
in us who walk not by the flesh but by the Spirit (Rom.
7 : 25 ; 8 : 3 f.)." That righteousness is not yet fulfilled
—and cannot be in this life—but it is on the way to
fulfilment. For it is God's work, as all living things
are. And He will complete it in His own time and
way.

And all the perplexing ethical problems to which
we referred earlier—are they solved ? By no means.
The whole justification for that earlier discussion was
that they are continuing problems, implicit in our
situation as finite, sinful men in a society in which
good and evil are so mixed. But in the measure we
yield ourselves to the forgiving and renewing love of
God in penitence and faith, relying not on ourselves
but on Him, we shall grow in wisdom as well as in
love. There is a kindly light to lead, though only one
step at a time, through a darkness which in large part
must remain impenetrable. To those who seek in
faith God will give light for each day's walking.

This seeking in faith is prayer, and the practice of
it is the discipline of the spiritual life. God can do
much for us without any recognition on our part that
He is the Doer and the Giver : He sends His rain upon
the just and the unjust and causes His sun to shine

upon the praying and the unpraying. But His most precious gifts, forgiveness and the renewal of life within, even God cannot bestow without our asking. And by "asking" is not meant a mere form of words, but a looking to God with faith and hope for what we know we need so desperately that the whole meaning of our existence depends upon the bestowal of it.

Except in occasional circumstances, in which one stands inescapably confronted with God and one's ultimate need, this "asking" cannot be done without discipline. There is a sense in which one can *never* pray unless one is *always* praying. The reason this is true is suggested by the fact that many of our beliefs are not the creative or revolutionary beliefs they would seem to be because we do not hold them vividly enough in our consciousness. I may believe, for example, that a certain cause deserves my fullest loyalty and support, but that belief will not determine to any great extent my character and life unless I frequently remind myself of it, meditate often on its significance, and renew my inner commitment to it. Otherwise, the fact that the cause is worthy of my allegiance (no matter how true) cannot have its full and proper effect. Likewise I may believe in God. I may believe that He, the Ground of my existence, is holy love, which both judges me, a sinner, and stands ready to redeem me. But unless I frequently—yes, constantly—contemplate the meaning and implications of that belief, make it my very own, yield myself to it, the belief cannot be a saving faith.

But the analogy has already broken down, for prayer is not meditation upon a belief; it is communion with Him to whom the belief relates. It is not a yielding of one's self to an idea, but to God. There is no such thing as a "saving faith"; only God saves. Prayer is our effort to give God the fullest possible opportunity to do for us and in us His forgiving, cleansing, creative work. It is thus not simply or only *our* seeking. It is a response to God's seeking of us. It is an active waiting before Him in penitence and faith. Such prayer is always answered. It is itself an answer to Him who stands constantly at the door and knocks.

VII.   THE SUSTAINING COMMUNITY

THROUGHOUT this chapter we have been thinking primarily of the individual Christian, with particular reference to his moral problem and the moral resources available to him. But there is a sense in which the phrase " individual Christian " is self-contradictory, for the very term " Christian " presupposes a social reality. An individual is a Christian in virtue of his membership in an historical community. It is as a member of that community that he sees his moral problem, and it is largely through the life of that community that the grace of God in Christ is mediated to him. Thus we are brought at the end to some discussion of the Church.

Most Christians have become increasingly aware in recent years of the Church as an important element in their religious faith—not the Church as a hierarchy, or as the clergy, or even as an institution at all, whether local or denominational, but as a particular and highly distinctive kind of human community. It is in this sense that the term has often been used in this book. If I may speak for a moment quite personally : As I think back on my experience as a student in a fairly typical liberal Protestant seminary twenty years ago, I have the impression that very little was said either by professors or among students about the doctrine of the Church. We talked, to be sure, about churches, but not about the Church. As a matter of fact, most of us students would have denied that such a thing existed at all. We could see the importance of churches as centres of worship and fellowship and agencies of social reform and social service, but " the Church "—that lay outside the circle of either our knowledge or our interest.

I went to a seminary where we often repeated together the Apostles' Creed. There were a number of items in that creed which meant little to many of us, and the item about the Church was certainly one of them : " I believe in the holy Catholic Church." I now realize that the principal reason other items meant no more was that this item meant so little ; that belief in the Church in a sense underlies, supports, is presupposed in our belief in God the Father Almighty and in Jesus Christ, His only Son, our Lord ; that these phrases have meaning only in the context which the life of the community provides. But this realization has come to me only recently, as it has to thousands in our generation. And this has happened because the Church is actually too real and important to be forever ignored. Vital facts cannot be permanently forgotten, especially if they are facts about us, and the Church is not only a vital fact but it is also a fact about us Western men, although millions of us have forgotten it. There are two aspects in particular under which this fact has made itself known to us.

First, we have come to recognize that the Church in its truest, deepest sense is not a congregation nor all of the congregations together, not a denomination nor all of the denominations together, but that it is a great historical community, comparable to a great nation but greater than any nation and transcending nationality. The Church under one of its aspects is nothing narrower or less pervasive than a culture. Many who had almost forgotten it have come to realize afresh in recent years that they belong to that culture ; that they belong to it not in the way one belongs to an organization one chooses to join, but in the way one belongs to one's home or one's country, only more deeply and completely ; that their own intimate personal life has been largely formed by this community, and that they can be their truest, most authentic selves only as they become more truly and deeply a part of it.

Under the influence of a certain false ideal of what a man ought to be, many of us have fought against recognizing this fact about ourselves. We have grown accustomed to the idea that a person ought, as far as possible, to become a pure individual, emancipated from his heritage, independent of any culture or group loyalty. The true man, according to this understanding, is the great, free, lonely soul, a lordly critic and eclectic, creating his own private culture by choosing what he likes from all the cultures. For such a one " culture " is something that belongs to one, not something to which one belongs. But the only culture worthy of the name is the culture which is in some measure *there* for one to belong to. The kind of culture we make for ourselves is weak and thin—a poor thing and not even our own. For what are really our own, as we have seen, are not the things we possess but the things that possess us. Man is not free in the way a lord is free on his throne—only God is really free that way— but in the way a child is free in his home. One may, of course, enrich and enhance one's cultural heritage, but only those can remake their culture who have first been made by it. The man without a country is not a citizen of the world ; he has ceased to belong to the world at all. The recognition that the Church is a distinctive historical community to which one belongs in the same way one belongs to a country or a culture is involved in our recently acquired sense of the reality and the importance of the Church.

And we belong to this community in a profounder sense than we belong to any other. Our Christian

Q

heritage is our most important heritage ; that is, it has had more to do with making many millions of us the persons we are than any other element in our inherited social environment, and to dissociate ourselves entirely from it, if that were possible, would entail a more serious derangement of our personal life than would dissociation from, say, our American heritage in so far as it is not also Christian. To recognize this fact is to recognize the importance of the Church both as fact and idea—at any rate for us. It is part of what we mean when we say, " I believe in the holy Catholic Church."

But this is not all we mean. Indeed, we mean vastly more than this. We mean that this community has a quite objective value which no other community could have ; that it has this unique and saving value not for us only, who have been born and reared within or near her walls, but also for all men, to whom, regardless of race, or class, or other cultural heritage, her gates are open. We mean that God offers in and through the Church a revelation of Himself which is not elsewhere to be found. The ground for that view of the significance of the Christian community has been stated in other chapters of this book, especially in Chapter 3. If the revelation of God in Christ is of supreme moment for mankind, the Christian community is also supremely significant. For the revelation occurred only within the life of that community. God did not manifest Himself in Jesus alone, but in the life of the group which was formed about him and in whose creation he was himself the decisive factor. It was in Jesus *as known in the Church* that the fresh activity of God among men, which we call the revelation in Christ, occurred.

And that revelation is not merely remembered in the Church ; it is constantly present wherever there is genuine Christian fellowship. Common worship is the corporate adoration of the God who has there revealed Himself as holiness and love ; it is corporate confession in His presence of failure and sin ; it is the expression of a common need for forgiveness and healing and renewal, and of a common reliance upon His grace. The sacrament of the Lord's Supper has its primary significance not as a mere memorial of something that happened centuries ago, but rather as an outward symbol of the fact that the God of truth and grace, of nature and history, who made Himself known in the life of the group which Christ called into being, is constantly making Himself known afresh in the life of the Christian community. The Church is not the relic of the Incarnation, but the continuation of it. It is this we mean when we speak of it as the Body of Christ.

Thus when we say, " I believe in the holy Catholic Church," what we really mean is not that we believe in the Church itself in any absolute sense but that we believe in the God who has made Himself known to us within the Church—the God whom Christ revealed. We belong to the Body of Christ because we have been laid hold on by Christ. We feel a deeper devotion to this community than to any other human society because we have found God there, or rather God has found us there. We belong to the Christian com- munity because within that community the God and Father of our Lord Jesus Christ has made Himself known to our hearts as grace and truth.

Needless to say, God's revelation of Himself is not confined to the Church, even in the broad sense in which that term has been used in this discussion. God is the Father Almighty, Maker of heaven and earth, and from the beginning of time, in the silence, the mystery, the order, the beneficence of nature, in the sweetness of friendship and love, in the joy of creative work and in all the things of beauty in which

Q*

men's hearts delight, as well as in the terror of His
judgments upon men's selfishness and pride, God has
been seeking to make Himself known. And who is
prepared to set limits to the degree to which He has
succeeded in doing so ? Or who has the right to say,
" God cannot reveal Himself to others except in the
way He has made Himself known to me " ? One
thinks here especially of the Jewish community, with
which the Christian Church stands in such close and
essential relation. But although none of the authors
of this book is authorized to speak for the others, I
feel sure it is safe to affirm as a common faith the
conviction that as God revealed Himself most effectively
in the first century, so He does in the twentieth—in
the fellowship of contrite hearts united in devotion to
the God and Father of our Lord Jesus Christ. Into
that fellowship all are invited to come—or to return.
In that fellowship, transcending race, nation, culture
—yea, time and death—are forgiveness, guidance, and
strength for us and our children, the salvation which
each one of us and our world so desperately need.

INDEX